design & make

mounting and setting stones

design & make

mounting and setting stones

SONIA CHEADLE

For Florence

ACKNOWLEDGEMENTS

First and foremost I would like to thank all the designer-makers and contributors whose work is featured in this book, and the overwhelming number of people who took the time to send in images; the many offers that went unused are nonetheless much appreciated. Very special thanks go to Leonie, for her steadfast support and 'red pen' encouragement; to Rebecca, for her expertise in CAD; and finally to Tim, for his skill and professionalism at interpreting my scribbles.

DISCLAIMER

Everything written in this book is to the best of my knowledge and every effort has been made to ensure accuracy and safety but neither author nor publisher can be held responsible for any resulting injury, damage or loss to either persons or property. Any further information that will assist in updating of any future editions would be gratefully received. Read through all the information in each chapter before commencing work. Follow all health and safety guidelines and where necessary obtain health and safety information from the suppliers. Health and safety information can also be found on the internet about some products.

First published in Great Britain 2010
A&C Black Publishers
36 Soho Square
London W1D 3QY
www.acblack.com

ISBN: 978-1-4081-0912-0

A CIP catalogue record for this book is available from the British Library

Commissioning editor: Susan James
Project editor: Davida Saunders
Copy editor: Julian Beecroft
Page design: Evelin Kasikov
Cover design: Sutchinda Thompson
Illustrations: Tim Hutchinson
CAD illustrations: Rebecca Currant

This book is produced using paper that is made from wood grown in managed, sustainable forests. It is natural, renewable and recyclable. The logging and manufacturing processes conform to the environmental regulations of the country of origin.

Printed and bound by Star Standard, Singapore

Images:
half-title page **Louise O'Neill, Set of six stacking rings.** Round and marquise-cut tourmalines set in 18ct white gold. Photo: FXP Photography.
frontispiece **Kelvin Birk, Deluxe Ruby Ring.** 18ct yellow gold and oval ruby. Photo: Kelvin Birk.

Contents

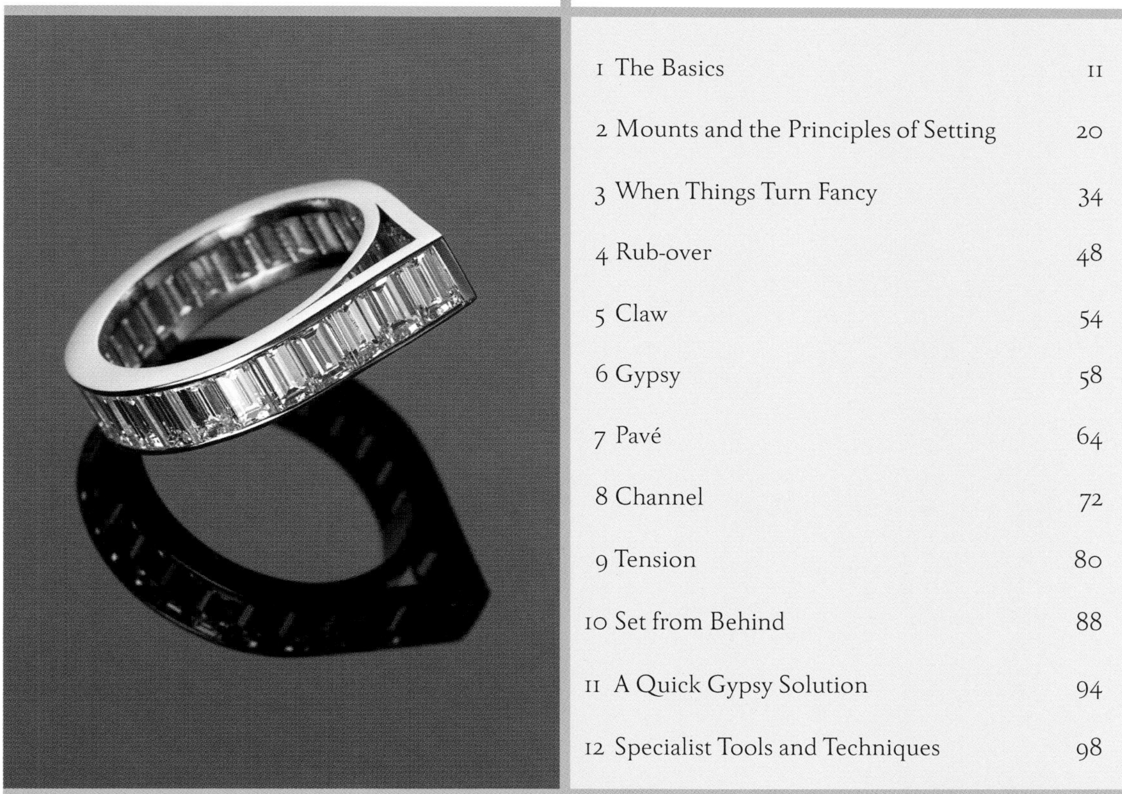

Sonia Cheadle, 90 Degrees of Eternity.
Platinum ring with channel-set diamonds. Photo: Robert Holmes.

Assorted gems. Courtesy of Marcia Lanyon Ltd. Photo: Andrew Scott.

preface
how this book came about

As a self-confessed magpie, with an eye for the more unusual, exciting and fancy-shaped gemstones, the time came after several years of collecting, to put some of my beautiful finds into items of jewellery. The journey started with an enquiry at the local bullion shop, and I still recall my horror at discovering that the mounts for such a varied collection of gems could not be bought. Embarrassed by my lack of knowledge even after four years studying jewellery making, I left sheepishly, the assistant's words ringing in my ears: 'The mounts for these stones will have to be individually made.'

Where on earth was I to begin? The enormous gap in my training was apparent; if I wanted to turn my collection into jewellery then I needed to learn the necessary techniques and processes.

Fortunately a postgraduate residency provided the opportunity and, more importantly, the time required to start this desperately needed research. With the luxury of a whole year under the guidance of a master setter, I was able to begin my discoveries.

It soon became apparent that mounting and setting were two different disciplines, each involving a distinct set of skills. As I had only one year of study available to me, I decided to focus on mount-making while building up a good relationship with the master setter. I realised that an expert setter can easily set a precise and accurately constructed mount.

After a year of scoring, folding, filing, bending and soldering the tiniest amounts of sheet metal, I had finally grasped the art of mount construction, while to set the stones in place I gladly employed the expertise of my new friend the master setter. Some people would view this as cheating; I see it as acknowledging someone else's area of expertise, as well as making sense in terms of time and cost. Besides, I did not have another year to spend perfecting the art of setting.

During the past ten years I have developed my skills and shared the experience I acquired with students at a variety of educational establishments as well as at my own jewellery school. Now, by imparting my expertise via a book, I hope to save many more of you years of frustrating trial and error.

This book is best viewed as a guide. Being the result of ten years of experiment, discovery and learning, it should not be taken as a set of fixed rules. After all, there is more than one way to cook an egg.

introduction

what this book is about

This book outlines a selection of setting styles, from the basic to the more complex, and looks at the mounts and setting techniques required for each specified style. The main purpose of the book is to aid a better understanding of mount construction and deliver the principles behind the outlined setting techniques in the hope of clarifying the mystique that often shrouds them both.

who this book is for

This book is intended for like-minded hoarders of precious stones as well as any jeweller wishing to explore and experiment within the world of mounting and setting.

It has been designed with the intermediate jeweller in mind, as a basic knowledge of jewellery making is required to carry out the techniques demonstrated. However, whether it is your first attempt at a rub-over, or you just want to know the ins and outs behind gypsy setting either as an established practitioner or a jewellery novice, there should be something for you here.

If you are relatively new to jewellery making, the glossary at the back is designed to explain unfamiliar jewellery terms and help clarify any trade jargon you may find in the book.

how to use this book

The first chapter of this book, The Basics, starts by taking a quick look at the jewellery industry as a whole then helps to outline and define the difference between the terms mounting and setting.

If you are new to working with stones then this would be a good place to start, and, for the seasoned professional, where is the harm in a quick recap?

The following two chapters, Mounts and the Principles of Setting and When Thing Turn Fancy, strip back the theory of mounting and setting with a closer look at how the stones relate to their mounts.

Each of the succeeding chapters focuses on a specific setting style. Through step-by-step demonstrations and stripped-down illustrations each chapter offers an overview of the specified style, followed by a guide to the mount construction and a review of the processes and techniques required to set the stones in place.

1. the basics

the industry as a whole

The jewellery industry involves thousands of people working in a large number of specialist areas. Designing, modelling, casting, enamelling, polishing and plating are but a few of them.

In order to attain the high standards required these craftsmen and women must undergo years of intensive training through institutions or apprenticeship schemes before they can be regarded as an expert within their chosen field.

Realistically, it would be impossible to become a master in every area of activity. For a designer-maker working with gemstones, however, it can prove invaluable to have a firm understanding of the specialist processes and techniques involved.

The two main disciplines that are the focus of this book are those of mounting and setting.

what is the difference between mounting and setting?

Mounting and setting are distinct terms that denote two entirely different processes. The two are often confused and taken, wrongly, to mean the same thing.

It is important, at this early stage, to clarify the difference between these two terms, as well as how they are referred to and used within the jewellery trade. The following quote from master setter David Basford should help us to identify and define these differences: 'The term *setting* refers to the fixing of precious stones into a metal ***mount*** using a variety of techniques and styles, the most basic of which has been used since ancient times. The setter works with a mount produced for this purpose in precious metals by the jeweller or silversmith.'

To summarise, metal surrounding a stone is referred to as a *mount* and the action of securing the stone or stones in place is known as *setting*.

It is quite common these days for the jeweller or silversmith to construct their own mounts and then to employ the skill and expertise of a master setter.

The main aim of this book is to deliver a deeper appreciation of both of these terms, of the processes involved and the techniques that lie behind them, enabling the maker to practise with greater confidence.

The stones pictured opposite are an array of popular cabochon and faceted stones in a variety of round and fancy shapes. The term 'fancy' in the jewellery trade is used to describe all stones that are not round in shape.

From left to right, starting at the top: trillion cabochon, emerald-cut facet, oval facet, round cabochon, marquise cabochon, round facet, marquise facet, baguette facet, triangle cabochon, half-moon cabochon, square mirror cut or pyramid facet, pear facet, oval facet, cushion cabochon, bullet cabochon, heart facet, hexagonal facet, oval cabochon, taper cabochon slab and square facet.

Stone cuts. Courtesy of Marcia Lanyon Ltd.
Photo: Andrew Scott.

the stones

Dome

Girdle

Cross section of a cabochon stone.

Before looking at both of these processes in detail, let us take a closer look at the stones that are to be mounted and set.

Traditionally gemstone rough is fashioned into either cabochon or faceted stones.

Cabochon-cut stones are smooth-shaped stones with a highly polished surface, which, when set, glow like coloured water droplets. A few good examples would be amethyst, citrine, blue topaz and peridot. Cabochon stones have a flat or slightly bevelled bottom and a domed top. The division between these two parts is referred to as the girdle and is the widest part of the stone.

Mark Nuell, high-dome pink tourmaline ring. 18ct yellow gold. Photo: FXP Photography.

Mark Nuell, series of ear studs.
18ct yellow gold with pink and blue sapphires. Photo: FXP Photography.

Faceted stones have many tiny flat faces that allow light to enter and be reflected back to the viewer, creating a sparkling affect. Traditionally, transparent forms of stones such as diamonds, rubies and sapphires are faceted to enhance their brilliance. However, translucent and even some opaque stones can also be cut in this way.

A faceted stone is also made up of two sections. The top of the stone is known as the crown while the bottom is referred to as the pavilion, and like the cabochon these two parts are separated by a girdle.

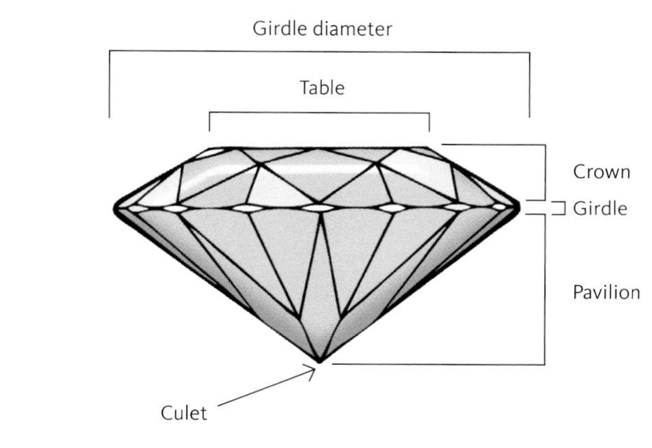

Cross section of a faceted stone.

Today the majority of gemstones are cut as both cabochon and faceted stones, and recent years have seen a succession of developments whereby modern technology has adapted traditional practice to create a whole new genre of cutting styles. The buff-top facet, the laser-cut chequerboard and the fabulous millennium cut are all direct results of these developments.

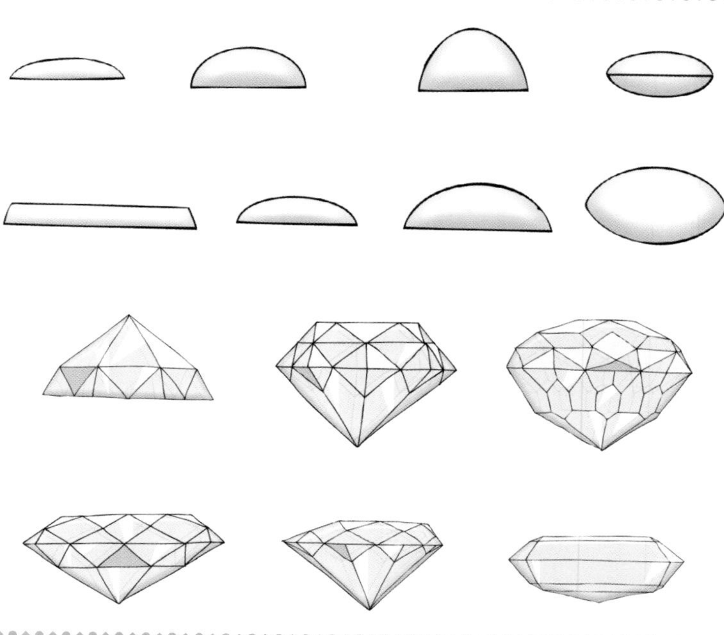

Cabochon and faceted profiles.

As well as differing in shape, the profiles or cross sections of stones can vary greatly too (as seen above). This is of paramount importance when working with gemstones, as the final height of a mount is always dictated by the curve or profile of a cabochon stone or by the depth of a faceted one.

POSITIONING THE STONE

Now we know more about cabochon and facet-cut stones our next concern is the positioning of the stone inside its mount. It will help to have a broader understanding of the mechanics and theory of how a mount works for each type of stone.

Traditionally, a cabochon stone sits in its mount with the dome up. A faceted stone sits with its crown up and its pavilion down.

Fortunately, for every form of mount or style of setting one factor remains constant. Whether a claw, channel, grain, tension or rub-over, it is always the girdle of the stone that is trapped by the metal of the mount. All mounts also work on a single principle, whereby a 'bearer' wire or ledge is prepared on the inside of the mount for the girdle of the stone to rest on. The metal of the mount is then pushed over or rubbed down onto the girdle to secure the stone in place.

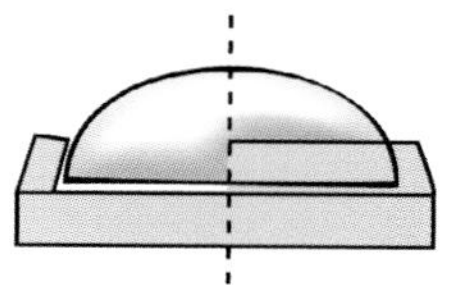

Cabochon and facet seated in a mount.

the bearer

Now let us take a closer look at the bearer itself. There are several ways in which a bearer can be created. A cross section and brief explanation of four variations is set out below:

Bearer one is used for cabochon stones only. In this case, the base of sheet metal, soldered to the bottom of the mount, acts as the bearer for the stone. The metal wall that forms the mount is often 0.5mm thick and is measured to fit closely around the stone.

Bearer two can be used for either cabochon or faceted stones. As in the above example a strip of metal is fashioned to encircle the girdle of the stone, but this time the bearer is formed from a small wire support which is soldered onto the inside of the mount.

Bearer three can also be used for both cabochon and faceted stones and there are two ways that it can be constructed.

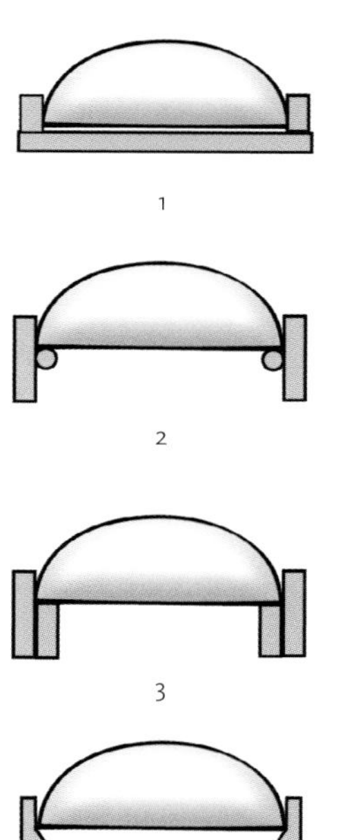

Cross sections of bearer types.

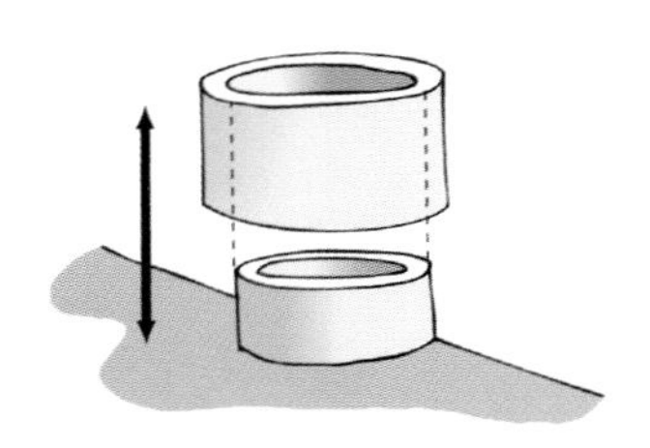

Inner and outer mount.

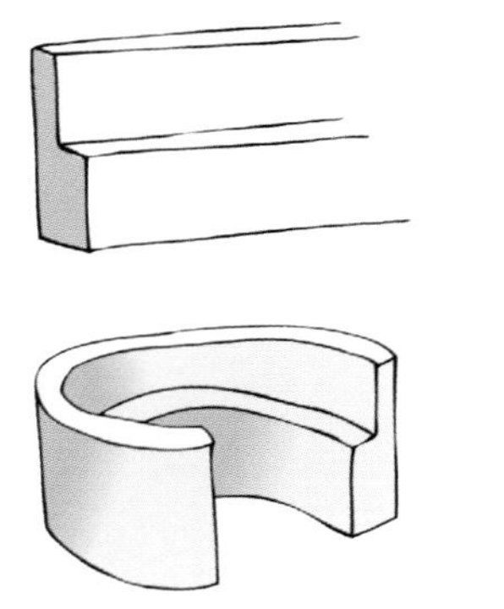

L-shaped strip.

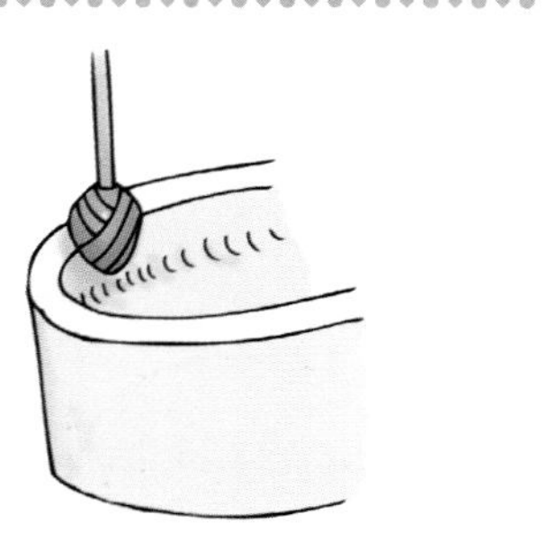

Burring bearer four.

Construction one: A mount is made to fit around the stone and a second mount is made to fit exactly inside the first. The two are then tapped together and soldered in place. The 'inner' mount, being shorter in height, creates the bearer.

Construction two: Two metal strips of different widths are sweat-soldered one on top of the other, creating an L-shaped cross section. The mount is then formed with the narrower strip on the inside to create the bearer. Because the bearer is already in position, only one mount need be made to encircle the stone.

Bearer four can be used for both cabochon and faceted stones, and because of its versatility and ease of construction is probably the most widely used of the four bearers outlined here. A single mount is formed from strip metal 0.8mm thick. The stone is required to sit on top of this mount and not inside, so that, when viewed from above, a clear wall of metal, known as a 'knife-edge', is visible around the whole of the stone's girdle. Using a steel burr and pendant motor, metal is then gradually removed from the inside of the mount. This creates the bearer ledge inside the mount on which the stone sits.

As in all of the examples, the bearer has to be below the surface of the mount, but there is no exact science to calculating its precise position. The following suggestions can, however, be used as a guide.

- For cabochon stones the depth of the bearer inside the mount is dictated by the curve of the domed top.
- For smaller faceted stones with a diameter of 1–2.5mm, the bearer should be positioned so that the table of the stone sits almost flush with the top of its mount.
- For larger-faceted stones, 2.6mm in diameter or more, the bearer should be positioned so that the top of the mount covers approximately one third of the crown.
- For both cabochon and faceted stones, if the bearer is too deep there will be too much metal to rub over and the stone will appear to be swallowed. If the bearer is too shallow, the girdle will not be held securely.

CALCULATING THE METAL NEEDED TO MOUNT A ROUND STONE

With regard to bearers one, two and three (on p.17–18), the mounts described fit around the circumference of the stone's girdle. To calculate the amount of metal required to make the mount, multiply the diameter of the round stone by 3.145 (π) and then add twice the thickness of the metal being used.

For example, the metal needed to mount a round stone with a diameter of 8mm with a mount thickness of 0.5mm would be calculated as follows:

8 x 3.145 = 25.16mm
25.16mm + (0.5 x 2) = 26.16mm

When using bearer four (on p.18), however, it is not necessary to add the thickness of the metal to the circumference measurement because we want the stone to sit on top of its mount and not inside. So the sum for an 8mm round stone in this example would be:

8 x 3.145 = 25.16mm

Now we known more about gemstones and their varying shapes and cuts, and we understand in more detail the function of the bearer, let's take a closer look at the mounts themselves.

TIP

When precision is of the utmost importance it is a good idea to round up measurement figures to the nearest whole number. This will allow for minor adjustments to be made. Remember, it is far easier to make a mount a fraction smaller than it is to make one a touch bigger.

2. mounts and the principles of setting

mounts

There are two main types of mount, the straight-sided mount and the conical. The main difference between the two lies in their cross section. Both types of mount can vary greatly in design, from the extremely plain to the ultra-elaborate. A plain straight-sided mount gives a strong sturdy feel to a piece of jewellery, whereas an elaborate conical mount creates elegance and a sense of light and space.

A STRAIGHT-SIDED MOUNT

Straight-sided mounts are best likened to small metal boxes constructed to echo the shape of a stone. Once the bearer is formed and the stone seated, the wall of the metal box is pushed down onto the girdle to secure the stone in place. Straight-sided mounts can be used for both cabochon and faceted stones. They have a strong contemporary feel and are regularly found in modern jewellery designs.

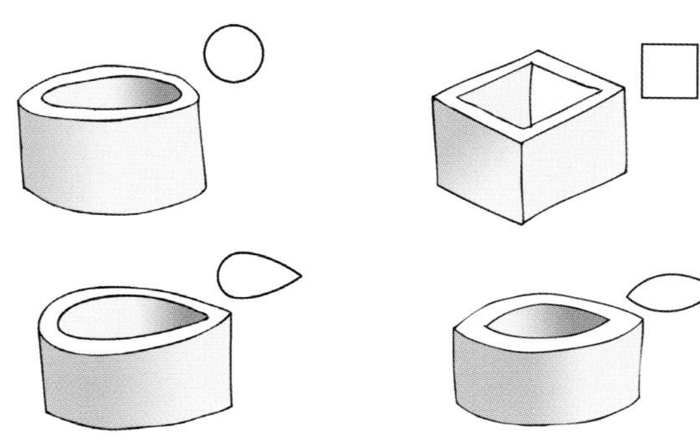

Straight-sided mounts.

A CONICAL MOUNT

Conical mounts have a tapered cross section similar to a miniature metal ice-cream cone. Once again, they are constructed to echo the shape of a stone, and the wall of the mount is pushed down onto the girdle to secure the stone in place. Conical mounts are more commonly used to set faceted stones and tend to be associated with a more traditional style of jewellery.

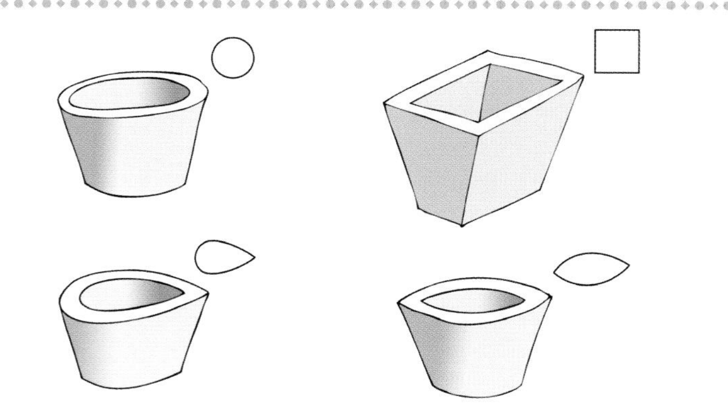

Conical mount.

READY-MADE MOUNTS

Both straight-sided and conical ready-made mounts can be bought 'off the peg' from the larger bullion and tool suppliers. It is a good idea to see which mounts are available to buy and whether they can be incorporated into your own jewellery designs. A word of warning: the majority of ready-made mounts are made to fit the more popular standard shapes and cuts – such as round, square, oval and emerald-cut – and they are usually cast in potentially expensive 18ct gold and platinum.

As well as ready-made mounts a large selection of metal tubing, known as chenier, can also be bought. Chenier is ideal material for making mounts because it is formed by extrusion, which, like casting, results in a seam-free, solder-free length of tube – so no more pesky leaking solder joins. However, the majority of commercially available chenier is round in shape and is made from silver, with only a few bullion suppliers stocking a variety of cross sections. Gold chenier tends to be extruded in the more simple shapes of round and square and in smaller dimensions.
Two suppliers worth a look are Rashbel and Bellore, both in Hatton Garden in London (see p.119).

The value of knowing how to construct your own mounts should be clear by now. Such knowledge will enable you to be more adventurous when selecting and purchasing gemstones and using the metal of your choice for your jewellery designs.

Let's take a look at the processes involved in constructing your own mounts.

ACCURACY IS KEY

When constructing either a straight-sided or conical mount, accurate measuring, precision scoring and exact folding are all key aspects to a successful build. However the real secret in achieving this lies in the tools we use. An early investment in a few well-engineered tools can save time and make even the trickiest tasks easier to accomplish. In addition to your basic toolkit, four such items regularly used in mount-making would be a well-balanced set of dividers, a well-defined small steel rule, a finely pointed steel scriber and a 2-cut 8-inch square needle file.

Secondary only to the tools themselves is the manner in which we use them. Accuracy and precision come with repetition and practice, and a slow considered approach is often far more beneficial than a hurried one. Unless you are very experienced, working quickly rarely saves time, as you are more likely to be inaccurate. If one piece of advice can be offered, make a conscious effort to slow down every stage of the construction process.

THE IMPORTANCE OF MEASURING

Whether straight-sided or conical a mount is always built according to the dimensions of the stone, so it is essential that the stone is measured correctly. A slight miscalculation can render the mount unusable which, when working in precious metals, can prove quite costly.

A mount for a round stone is by far the easiest to construct, as even the most basically equipped workshop will have an abundance of cylindrical objects that can be used as formers. Knowing this, let's keep things simple and start by looking at the construction for both straight-sided and conical mounts for a round stone. Once the basic construction techniques for a round mount are understood, the principles can be adapted to more complex and fancy-shaped stones.

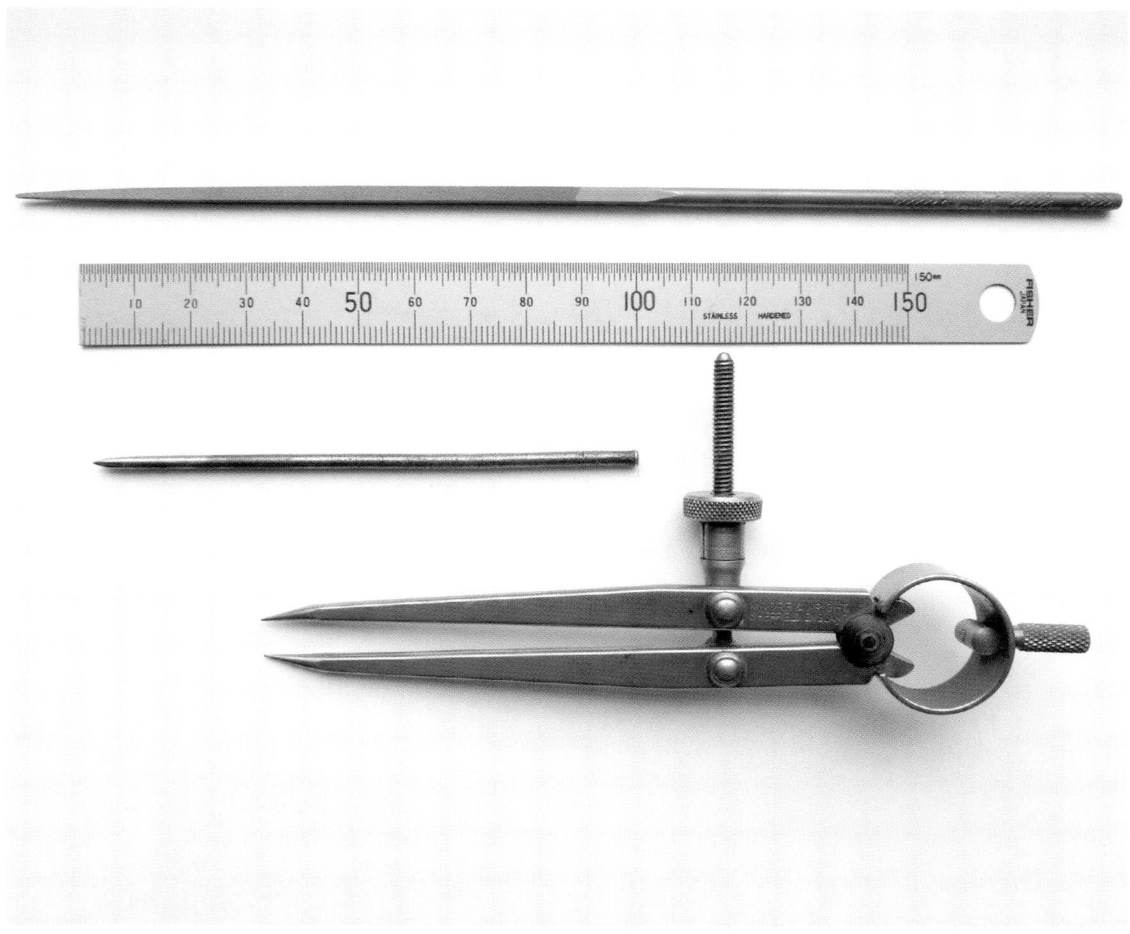

Dividers, rule, scribe and square needle file. Photo: Sonia Cheadle

Measuring diameter and depth with a micrometer (above) and steel rule (below).
Photo: Sonia Cheadle.

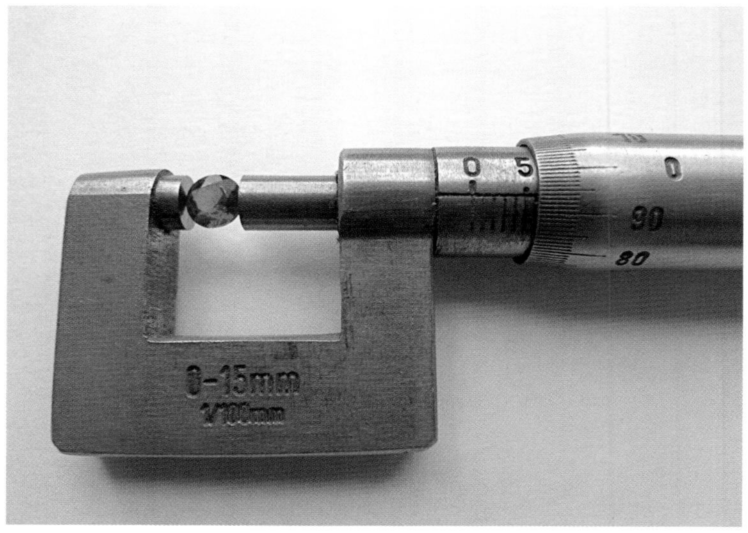

DIAMETER AND DEPTH

The two measurements of importance at this stage in the construction process are diameter and depth. A stone-measuring gauge is the easiest way to take these measurements, although such gauges can be expensive. However, a micrometer, a vernier gauge or even a well-defined steel rule can be just as effective and a lot less costly. Once these two measurements are known, the construction can begin.

CALCULATING A ROUND STRAIGHT-SIDED MOUNT

For this example, a 16mm round black onyx cabochon has been chosen. The mount strip will be made of silver with a thickness of 0.6mm. The bearer for this example will be bearer one, as described in Chapter 1 (p.17).

First, the height of the mount needs to be determined. As seen in the photograph (opposite), this measurement depends on the curve of the cabochon's domed top. For this example, a mount with a height of 4mm would be suitable, to accommodate the stone as well as to account for metal loss during the construction process.

Now the height of the mount has been established, the next step is to calculate the length of metal strip required to fit the circumference of the stone's girdle. First, multiply the diameter of the stone by 3.145 (π), then, because on this occasion the stone is required to sit inside its mount, add to this number twice the thickness of the metal strip. If this equation is not applied then the mount will be too small for the stone.

For example:

16 x 3.145 = 50.32mm
50.32mm + (0.6 x 2) = 51.52mm

The dimensions of the strip should therefore be:
4mm x 52mm x 0.6mm

CONSTRUCTING A ROUND STRAIGHT-SIDED MOUNT

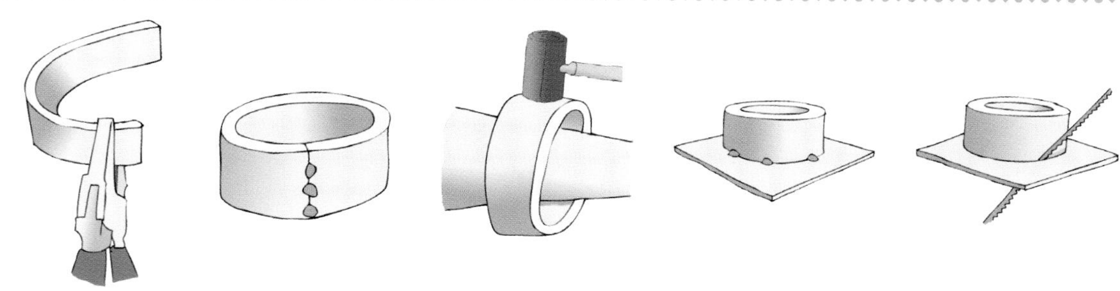

Now we have the correct length of strip the mount can be constructed according to the following steps:

- ▶ Evenly anneal the metal strip, cool and pickle.
- ▶ Using a pair of half-round pliers form the strip into a circle, taking care to keep the sides of the circle parallel.
- ▶ Meet the ends in a good join and solder the seam with hard silver solder. Cool and pickle.
- ▶ True the mount into a perfect circle on a steel triblet using a hide mallet.
- ▶ With a hand file, remove any excess solder from the seam and level both the top and bottom of the mount.
- ▶ Remove all file marks using emery paper either on a flat stick or fixed into the split pin of a pendant motor.
- ▶ Check the mount for size, as it is easier to adjust the mount at this stage, before the base is in place.
- ▶ Solder the mount onto a sheet silver base. Cool and pickle.
- ▶ Pierce around the base following the wall of the mount.
- ▶ File true and emery-paper the whole mount to a fine finish.

Now the mount is complete, the next step is to incorporate it into the item of jewellery or silverware, seat the stone on its bearer and prepare the piece for setting.

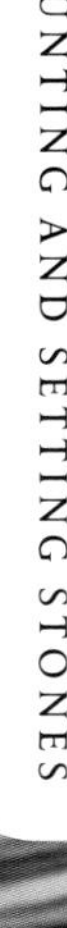

CALCULATING A ROUND CONICAL MOUNT

For this example, a 10mm round, faceted cubic zirconia has been chosen. The mount will be made from sheet silver with a thickness of 0.8mm. In a conical mount, the sloping wall can be used as a bearer, though it is advisable to create a definite seat for the stone, using either a steel burr and pendant motor or a graving tool. This will stop the stone from tipping and rolling during the setting process.

As before, the first measurements required are the diameter and depth of the stone being used. For this example the diameter is known to be 10mm and the depth of the stone from culet to table is 6mm, measured using a micrometer.

There is one important difference between the construction of a conical mount and that of a straight-sided one. Instead of a straight metal strip, one with a slight curve is needed to give a cone-shaped cross section, and our concern here is how to achieve this. There are several ways to form this curve, and with the diameter of the stone known and the depth of the mount decided, let us move on to scribing a template that can be used when a curved strip of metal is required.

Visible culet.

TIP

In a conical-shaped mount the pavilion of a faceted stone should be completely enclosed by the mount. It is important to allow for this when calculating the height of the mount, a mount too shallow may result in the culet poking out through the back of the mount after setting. This in turn can cause discomfort when the jewellery item is worn, especially in the case of rings.

To understand the diagram (opposite) a couple of points need to be noted. One is that the cross section of the conical mount is being built upside down; the second is that the angles of a collet block and former, used to true the mount during construction, are usually machined with either 17° or 28° taper. Remembering this should help when mapping in the sides of the mount.

- First scribe the line AB. This is equal to the diameter of the stone, in this case 10mm, and will indicate the top of the mount.
- Half way along AB, in this case at 5mm, extend a line upward and perpendicular to create the centre line.
- Mark the height of the mount on the centre line, in this case 8mm, and scribe in a line running parallel to AB. This line indicates the base of the mount.
- Now we need to plot the first side of the mount. Using A as a starting point, take a steel rule, angled at approximately 17° or 28°, and scribe the line OA. O is the intersection where this line crosses the centre line.
- The second side of the mount can now be scribed to form OB.
- The cross section, indicated by the dark shaded area, now has to be extended to create the template.
- Set a pair of dividers with the radius OB and extend a long arc.
- Close the dividers to match the measurement OC and scribe a second arc.
- Multiply the diameter of the stone by 3.14 (π) and add twice the thickness of the metal strip.
  So: 10 x 3.14 = 31.4mm 31.4 + (0.8 x 2) = 33mm
- 33mm is the length of metal required to fit the circumference of the stone, and needs to be plotted along the first arc. This then creates the top of the template, BD.
- To complete the template, connect OD.
- The lighter shaded area is then pierced out and used to construct the conical mount.

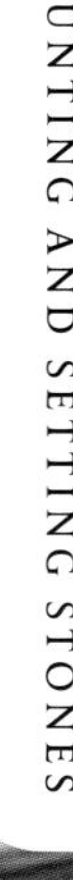

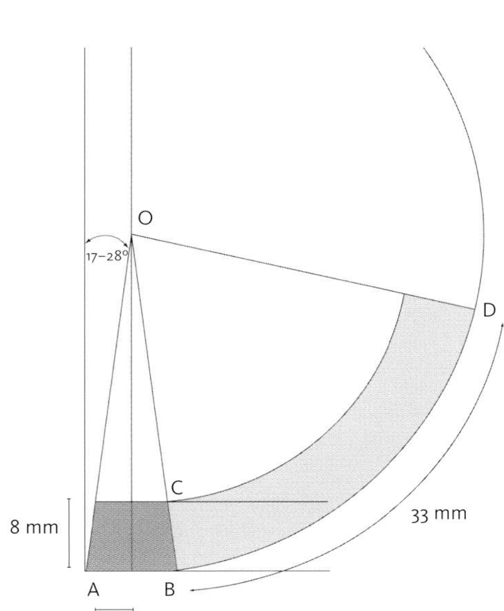

Conical template.

When making a conical mount from precious metal, avoid any unnecessary expense and metal wastage by first making a master template out of base metal. Then, using the master, calculate the dimensions required for a precious version. This way you will only buy the exact amount of precious metal you need.

CONSTRUCTING A ROUND CONICAL MOUNT

Now we have our curved strip of metal, take the following steps to manipulate it into a conical mount:

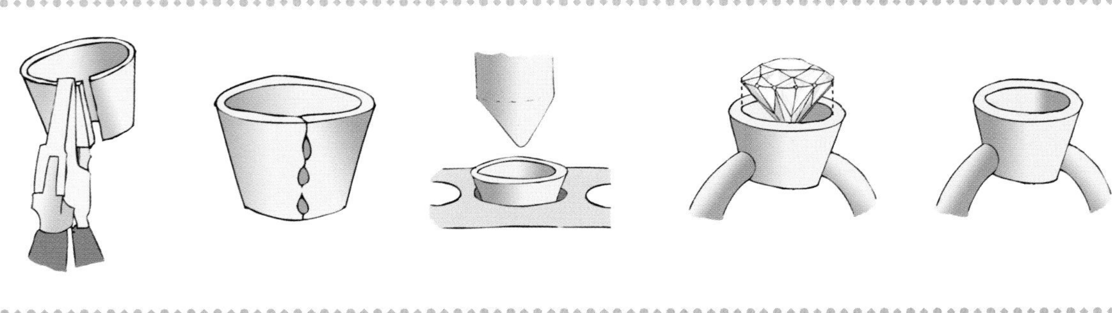

- Evenly anneal the curved strip, cool and pickle.
- Using a pair of snipe-nosed pliers, form the strip into a cone taking care to keep the top and bottom of the strip parallel.
- Meet the ends in a good join and solder the seam with hard silver solder. Cool and pickle.
- True the mount in a steel collet block by tapping the male former with a hide mallet.
- Using a hand file, remove any excess solder from the seam and level both the top and bottom of the mount.
- Remove all file marks using emery paper either on a flat stick or fixed into the split pin of a pendant motor.
- Check the mount for size, as it is easier to make a small adjustment at this stage.
- File true and emery-paper the whole mount to a fine finish.

With the mount now complete, the next step is to incorporate it into the item of jewellery, create the bearer to seat the stone and prepare the piece for setting.

the principles of setting

Like a well-choreographed dance routine, there are only a few basic steps you need to remember when it comes to setting stones, yet the order in which they are performed is crucial to the end result.

The majority of setting styles are born of the main two, the rub-over and the claw. Either applied individually or combined to create an elaborate hybrid, they share the same principles and utilize the same tools and techniques.

The main concern in this section is to outline the basic principles common to all the setting styles. The chapters that follow will examine and explain individual setting styles in greater detail.

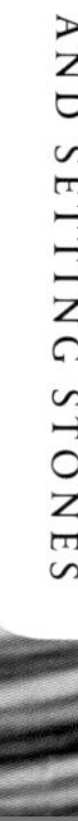

TOOLS

A setter's bench is laid out in much the same way as that of a jeweller. They both have a semicircular recess to allow close proximity to the working area, a bench skin to catch metal filings, and a good overhead light source. One significant difference, however, is the bench peg. A setter's peg is shorter in length than that of a jeweller's, and instead of a split running front to back, a curve is carved from left to right. This curve is essential to supporting the body of a setting stick during the setting process. If you want to set your own stones on a regular basis, it is advisable to have a pair of interchangeable pegs.

Some of the tools needed to set stones are: graving tools, Arkansas stone and oil, setting sticks, steel burrs, push tools, safety back file, buff stick and a pendant motor – not forgetting good eyesight and upper-body strength, as setting can be a very demanding physical activity.

The setter's bench pictured below is typical. The curved peg can clearly be seen and the selection of tools shown is that mentioned above.

Setter's bench and essential tools.

TIP

For a more detailed account of the processes involved in sticking up and removing a metal mount from a setting stick, alongside a guide on maintaining graving tools, see Chapter 12, Specialist Tools and Techniques.

TECHNIQUES

The secret to successful setting is the way in which each part of the process is carried out. It takes accuracy and precision to seat a stone correctly, whilst physical strength, concentration and care are required to set. Both will have a more successful outcome if the setter takes a slow and conscientious approach.

During the setting process the 'pushing' arm exerts an enormous amount of force. To counteract this pressure the setter must sit straight, have a strong 'holding' arm and be well braced throughout the process. Otherwise, a slip will occur and the stone may be damaged, scratched or gouged.

When seating a stone the bearer may need a slight adjustment so that the girdle of the stone sits straight and level. Steel burrs and a pendant motor or graving tools are used to achieve this. Some stones, mainly cabochons (and often the cheaper ones), have irregular and uneven girdles that sit on a slant. In this case the bearer may need to be burred a fraction deeper in some areas so as to account for the uneven line of the girdle. Once the stone is correctly seated, setting can begin. As with mount construction, the method for setting a round stone is by far the simplest, and once the basics are understood they can be adapted for fancy-shaped stones and other setting styles.

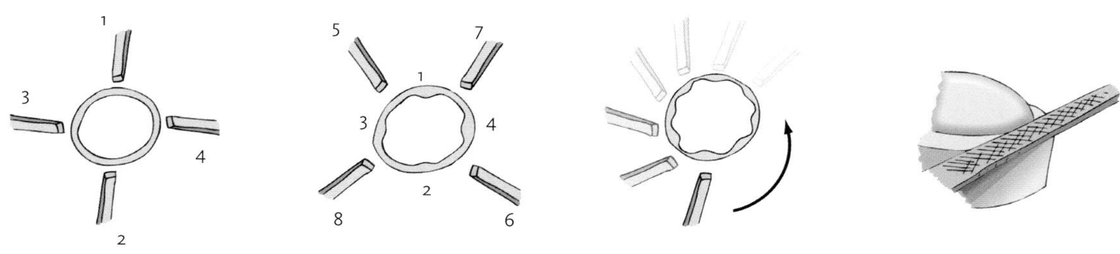

The rub-over method for setting a round cabochon stone using a flat-ended setting tool or push stick.

With the mount securely held in setter's wax, the stone is lightly tacked into place with the first four pushes. Viewing the stone as a clock face, the metal is pushed over at 12.00 and 6.00, then at 9.00 and 3.00. Work around the stone, easing the metal gently onto the stone, always pushing from opposing sides, as this action will help avoid a corrugated and uneven rim.

When the stone is secure, continue to work slowly round the rim of the mount to smooth out any lumps and bumps.

Finally file and emery the mount, taking great care not to scratch the stone.

TIP

Some stones are softer than others and will be easily damaged if caught by a file or piece of emery paper. Friedrich Mohs devised a scale as a guide to mineral strength and composition.
For a more detailed explanation of this scale, **see Chapter 12.**

3. when things turn fancy

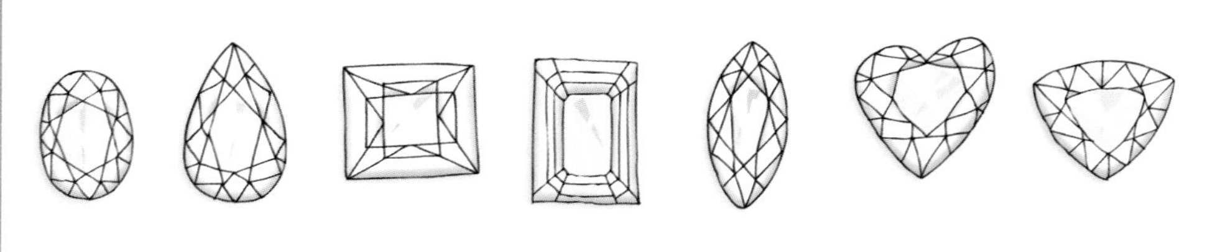

A selection of fancy-shaped, faceted stones.

As mentioned in the previous chapter the term 'fancy' in the jewellery trade is used to describe all stones that are not round in shape. The principles for making a fancy-shaped mount, whether straight-sided or conical, are the same as for a round one but, due to their shape, the construction techniques and tools used differ slightly, making the process a little more complex. When constructing a mount for a fancy-shaped stone the first challenge is finding the circumference of the stone. For a round stone this task is made simple by the application of pi (π); unfortunately there is no such formula for fancy-shaped stones, so let's start by looking at a couple of ways of finding the circumference of a few of the more common shapes.

Straight-sided stones such as square, baguette and triangle, pose little problem as the length of each side is easily measurable using a small, well-defined steel rule. Measuring the distance around the girdles of the more curvaceous stones such as oval, pear, trillion, marquise and heart, is less easy. One solution is to use a length of steel binding wire that, using a pair of snipe-nosed pliers, can be easily fashioned around the girdle. To record the circumference, you simply straighten out and measure the wire.

The second measurement needed when calculating the dimensions for the metal strip is the depth of the stone. This measurement can easily be found using a small steel rule, micrometer or vernier gauge as outlined in the previous chapter.

The above measurements provide us with the overall dimensions of the metal strip. This strip now needs to be subdivided so that it can be bent or soldered into the exact shape of the stone. Before we do this, we must consider how mounts for different-shaped stones are formed.

Traditionally a single length of metal strip is measured, scored and folded to form a fancy-shaped mount. This method works well for some makers yet frustrates others, and if you have ever attempted this then you will be fully aware of how difficult it can be, as the slightest miscalculation will result in a lopsided, unusable mount.

Fortunately, there is a simple solution, and that is to construct the mount in two halves, mitre each of them, then solder both halves together to complete. Genius – though there is one small catch. When opting for a mitred mount, the metal lost during the mitring process has to be accounted for when calculating the circumference and scoring the folds of the mount. Thankfully, this can easily be resolved by adding an extra 0.5mm length to each side when measuring the circumference of the stone, then remembering to account for it when setting dividers to score each fold.

TIP

When measuring symmetrical stones – for example, the marquise or heart – save time by measuring only one side of the stone then double the distance to find the circumference.

TIP

Using two pairs of pliers 'pull' the length of binding wire straight before shaping it around the stone. This action releases the tension from the binding wire, allowing a more precise shape to be formed.

Considering this, let us take a quick look at a few of the more commonly used fancy-shaped stones and suggest how their mounts might be constructed. In the illustration below, a single line denotes where the solder join is best placed for that particular mount, and two lines indicate a soldered mitre.

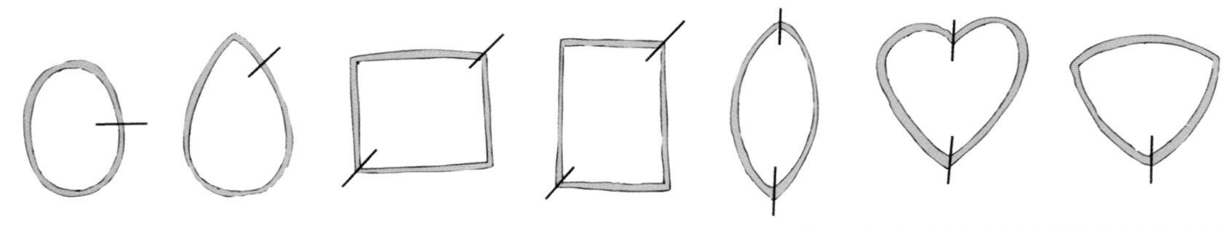

A selection of fancy-shaped mounts.

By this stage, we should be proficient at measuring the depth of a stone, be confident at how to resolve any circumference issues, and have a greater understanding of how a mitre can help with construction. To reinforce these procedures let's now look at the calculation, construction, seating and setting of a fancy-shaped mount.

straight-sided, fancy-shaped mounts

SQUARE FANCY

For this example we will be constructing a straight-sided mitred mount, for a 5mm square-faceted stone, using bearer four (see p.18). Because the stone is required to sit on top of the mount after construction, the metal strip needs to be 0.8mm thick.

▶ Calculate the dimensions for the metal strip, the length of which equals the total of all four sides of the stone plus an extra 2mm (0.5mm x 4) to account for metal lost in the mitring process. The width of the strip is calculated by measuring the depth of the stone. So for this example the dimensions of the metal strip are 22mm x 4mm x 0.8mm.

▶ Cut the strip into two equal lengths. To do this, open a pair of dividers to 11mm and, using the short edge of the strip to guide the dividers, mark and score a line. Pierce directly down this line.

▶ True each 'cut' end to a precise right angle using a hand file.

▶ Mark and score the centre line of each section by setting the dividers to 5.5mm and scribing as before. This time, do not pierce.

▶ File a right-angled channel down the centre lines. First drag a piercing blade through the scored line to help define and locate the channel. Once a definite groove has been formed, introduce the right-angled edge of a square needle file into the groove and slowly file the channel deeper. Filing must stop halfway through the thickness of the metal.

▶ Fold each section into a right angle. To do this hold one side of the channelled strip in a pair of parallel pliers, lean the other side against the bench and gently apply pressure, so as to close the channel and create a tight right-angled fold. Each right-angled section is then soldered to strengthen the fold.

▶ Mitre both halves of the mount. To do this take each right-angled section and, using a hand file, create a mitre by filing straight across the two short edges. Take great care to file the mitre even and straight, to ensure a close and accurate join.

▶ Assemble the mount by putting the two halves together. Hold them in place during soldering by forming a binding wire 'man' around the body of the mount. For details of how to do this refer to Chapter 12, Specialist Tools and Techniques. Once soldered, the construction process is complete. The mount is then incorporated into the jewellery item and prepared for setting.

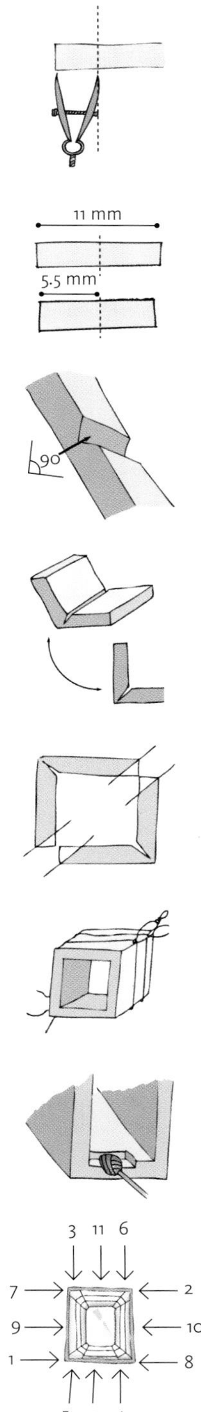

▶ Prepare the mount for setting by seating the stone. A stone-setting burr is slowly worked around the inside of the mount to create a bearer ledge to seat the girdle of the stone. When cutting a bearer for a fancy-shaped mount, start burring from the centre of one side and with slow and even strokes work the burr carefully into the corner. Turn the piece and repeat. Burring should stop when the stone sits level inside the mount and at 'optimum' depth. A knife-edge scorper can be used to true and define the bearer.

▶ For this example a 'rub-over'-style setting is used to secure the stone in place.

All the processes outlined above need to be executed with extreme accuracy and precision, and may require a number of attempts to perfect. If you are relatively new to jewellery making, do not be disheartened if your first few mounts are not exact. Stay relaxed, keep your focus and give it another go – after all, practice makes permanent as well as perfect.

Now we have mastered the square fancy, let us take a quick look at how to construct straight-sided mounts for a few more of our fancy-shaped friends.

BAGUETTE FANCY

The majority of baguette-cut stones have a length that is equal to twice the width – for example, 4mm x 2mm or 5mm x 2.5mm. The process of constructing a mitred mount for a baguette is the same as that for a square, and once again an extra 0.5mm is added to the length of each side to account for metal lost during the mitring process. Because the method of construction is identical to that of the square, once the correct lengths of strip have been cut, simply follow the steps outlined on p.37 and above for the construction process.

PEAR FANCY

The traditional construction method for a pear-shaped, straight-sided mount is to start forming the metal strip from the middle and bring the two ends to meet at the tip. This method can prove difficult, however, because the tip of the pear can vary considerably from a soft curve to a sharp point. The method outlined below overcomes this difficulty by suggesting that the tip of the mount is formed first; this way the tip of the stone can be mirrored exactly.

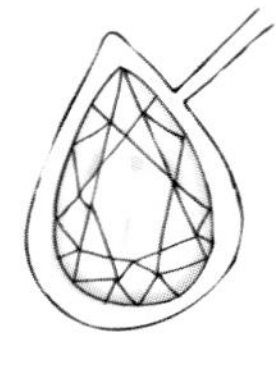

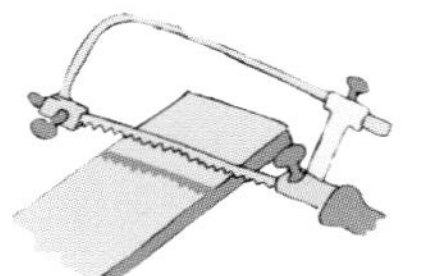

- ▶ Find the circumference of the stone using binding wire.
- ▶ Calculate dimensions for the mount strip and cut it out from metal 0.8mm thick.

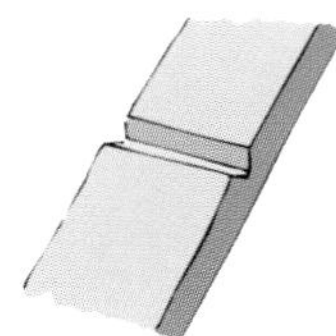

- ▶ True the ends of the strip with a hand file and, using a pair of dividers, score a line approximately 4mm along.
- ▶ Define the scored line with a piercing blade to form a groove.

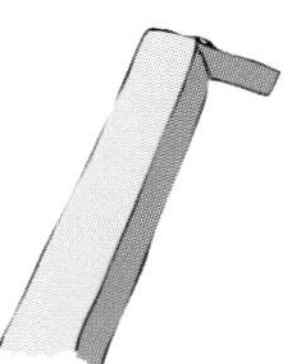

- ▶ Using a square needle file open out the groove into a channel.
- ▶ File the channel three quarters of the way through the thickness of the metal, as this time the angle required is greater than 90°.

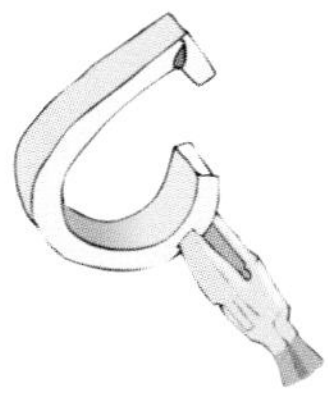

- ▶ Fold over the 4mm section of the strip to mirror the angle or curvature of the point of the pear, then solder to strengthen the fold.
- ▶ Hold the opposite end of the strip in a pair of snipe-nosed pliers and curl the strip round to form the body of the pear.

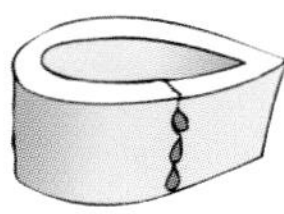

- ▶ Bring the ends together in a true join and solder the seam to complete the construction.

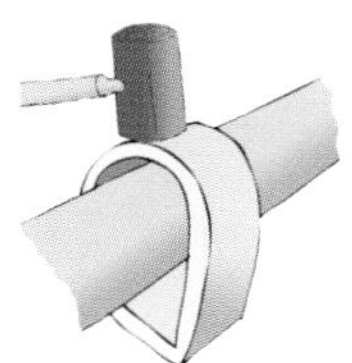

- ▶ True the shape of the mount using an appropriate-sized round former.

OVAL FANCY

The curves of oval-shaped stones can differ widely. So, to have more control over the final shape, start by making a round mount and, once construction is complete, use a pair of parallel pliers to ease the round into an oval.

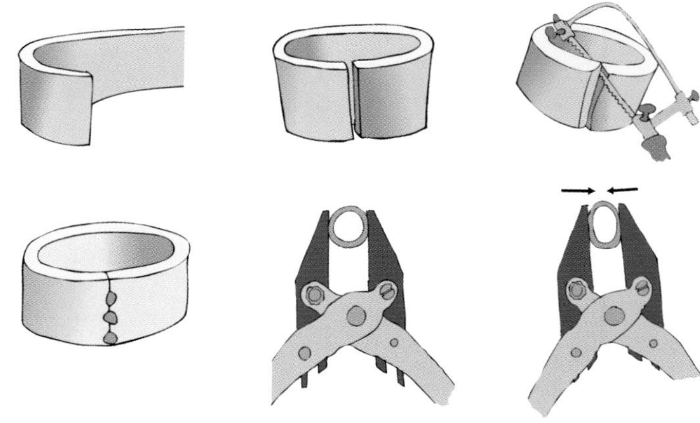

- Find the circumference of the stone using binding wire.
- Calculate the dimensions for the mount strip and cut it from metal 0.8mm thick.
- True the ends of the strip, then anneal, cool and pickle.
- Holding one end of the strip in a pair of snipe-nosed pliers, curl the strip round to form a semi-circle.
- Repeat the above step, working from the other end of the strip, to complete the circle.
- Bring the ends together and pierce through the join to ensure an accurate join.
- Solder the seam with hard solder
- True the mount on a suitable round former.
- Using a pair of parallel pliers, ease the mount into an oval shape.

MARQUISE FANCY

As with other symmetrical stones a mitred mount is ideal for the marquise, though the construction process is simpler than for right-angled stones as there is no need to file a channel.

As before, two identical halves of the mount are formed, mitred then soldered together; and as long as each step is executed with accuracy and precision, constructing a straight-sided marquise mount can be quite enjoyable.

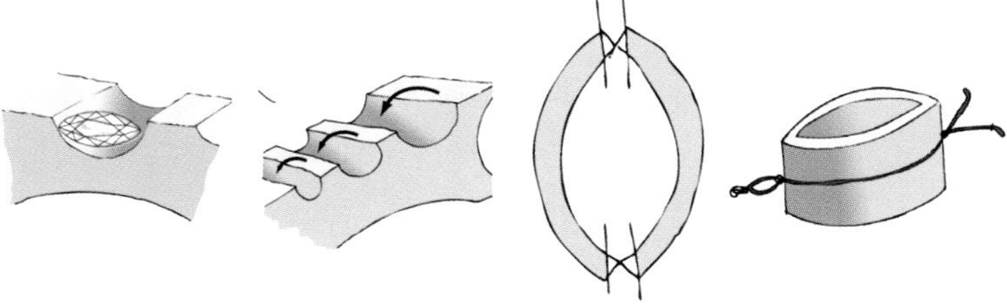

- Measure the circumference of the stone using binding wire, and, because the mount is to be mitred, remember to add the extra 0.5mm to each side.
- Calculate the dimensions of the marquise strip and cut from metal 0.8mm thick.
- Cut the strip into two equal sections using a piercing frame.
- True the ends with a file. Anneal, cool and pickle.
- Use a swage block and former to curve each section of strip; choose a recess that best echoes the shape of the stone.
- Mitre both halves of the marquise mount using a hand file. Take great care to file the mitre even and straight to ensure a close and accurate join.
- To complete the mount, solder the two halves together with hard solder, using a binding wire 'man' as a brace.

HEART FANCY

A heart-shaped mount also benefits from being mitred. As it is difficult to form two identical heart-shaped 'halves', it is best to form just one 'half' heart out of metal strip that is double the required width plus a little extra to allow for a piercing blade. The formed strip is then pierced straight down the middle of its width to create two identical halves.

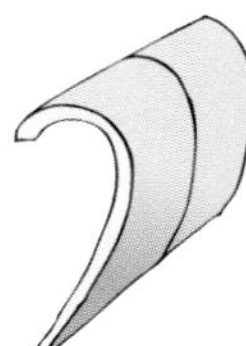
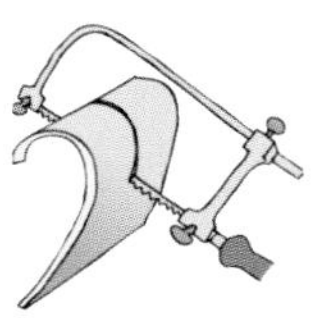

- ▶ Measure one half of the heart using binding wire; straighten out the length and record this distance. As it is to be mitred, add 0.5mm to this measurement.

- ▶ This time the width of the strip will be double the depth of the stone plus a little for the piercing blade, and the length will equal only one side of the heart. Calculate the dimensions of the heart strip and cut this from metal 0.8mm thick.

- ▶ Using a pair of dividers, scribe a central line down the length of the strip to indicate the individual 'heart' halves. Anneal, cool and pickle.

- ▶ With the scribed line on the outside, first form the indented top section of the heart by curling the edge of the strip inward using a pair of snipe-nosed pliers, then form the curve of half the heart using half-round pliers.

- ▶ Once the strip is formed to echo one half of the heart, pierce down the score line to create two identical halves.

- ▶ Mitre both halves of the heart mount using a hand file. Take great care to file the mitre even and straight, to ensure a close and accurate join.

- ▶ To complete the heart, solder the two halves together with hard solder, using a binding-wire brace.

TRILLION FANCY

A trillion-shaped mount is one of the more challenging mounts to make, as it is best suited to the traditional method of construction. To ensure a well-proportioned equilateral shape the strip has to be divided with great accuracy into three equal sections, and the dividing channels have to be carefully filed at right angles. When calculating the dimensions of the metal strip, add an extra 0.5mm to the length of each side, to take account of the fact that the angle of the fold is greater than 90° and is positioned on a curve.

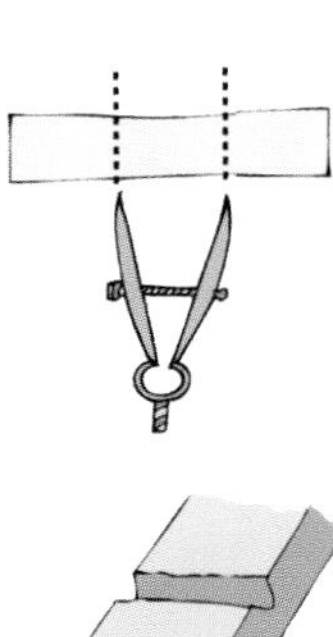

- Find the circumference of the stone using binding wire.
- Calculate the dimensions and cut the strip from metal 0.8mm thick.
- True the ends with a hand file. Anneal, cool and pickle.
- Open a pair of dividers to the length of one side of the trillion, remembering to add an extra 0.5mm.

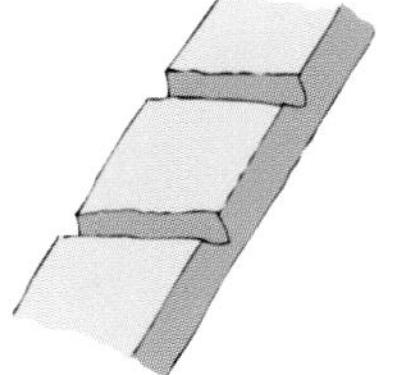

- Score this distance from one end of the strip. Define the score line using a piercing blade, then, using the defined groove to guide the dividers, score the second fold line. Define with a piercing blade.
- Using a square needle file, open out each groove to form a channel. This time the channel needs only to be cut one third of the way into the thickness of the metal.

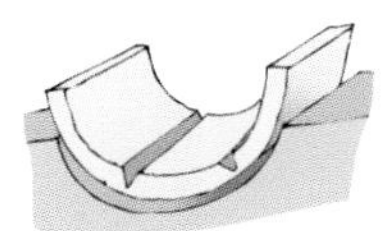

- Place the channelled strip into a large recess of the swage block, and choosing the appropriately sized former, ease the strip into a curve.

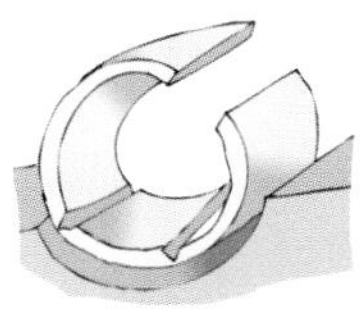

- Move the strip into a smaller recess of the block to encourage a tighter curve. Repeat this process until the curve of the strip follows that of one side of the stone.
- Anneal, cool and pickle.

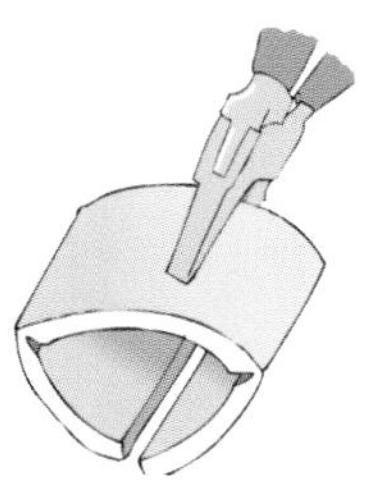

- Using a pair of half-round pliers, fold the outer sections of the strip toward each other until they meet. Pierce through the join to encourage a good seam.

- Form a binding wire 'man' around the body of the trillion. Solder all three corners using hard solder.

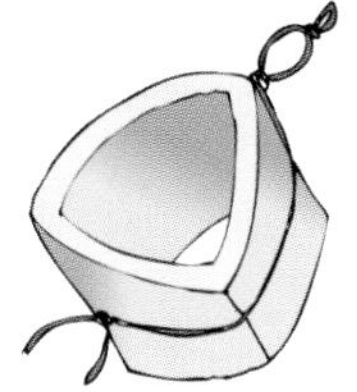

FORMING AN ACCURATE FOLD

When constructing fancy-shaped mounts the secret to creating an accurate fold lies in the process of filing the channel, and as every stroke of the file counts, a slow, steady and considered approach will return a better outcome. Problems can be encountered during filing, however, and the walls of the channel will reveal where things are going wrong.

All problems are due to human error, but once they have been identified we can work on correcting them. Often, something as simple as a slight change in seating position can make a huge difference.

The diagrams below will help identify and resolve a few of the common problems encountered whilst filing a channel.

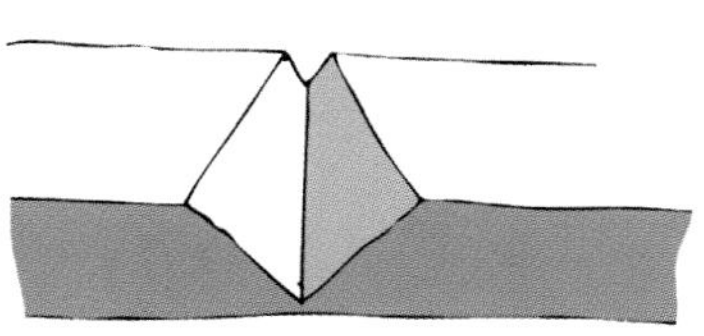

The walls of the channel indicate an 'uphill' filing action. To correct, lower the tip of the file by raising the wrist, then focus on pushing the file evenly through the channel.

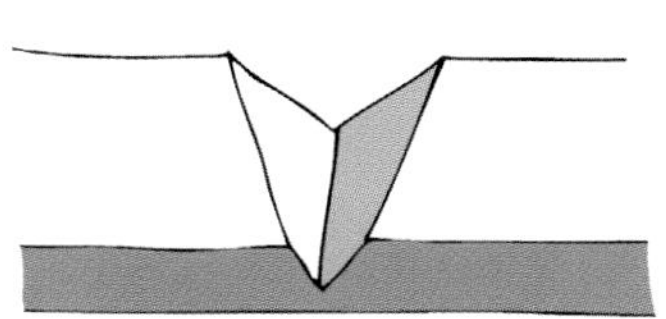

The walls of the channel indicate a 'downhill' filing action. To correct, lower the handle of the file by dropping the wrist slightly, then focus on pushing the file evenly through the channel.

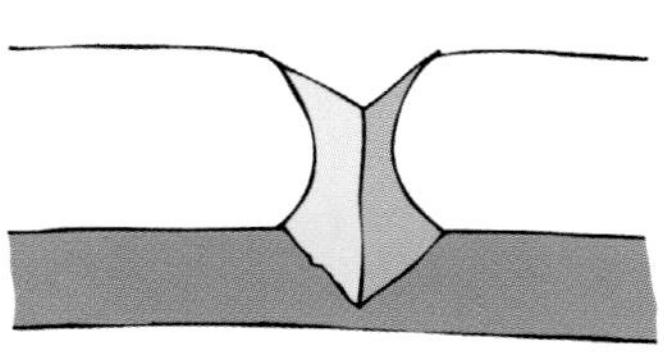

The walls of the channel indicate an 'hour-glass' filing action. To correct, steady the wrist to avoid pivoting during the forward stroke, then focus on pushing the file evenly through the channel.

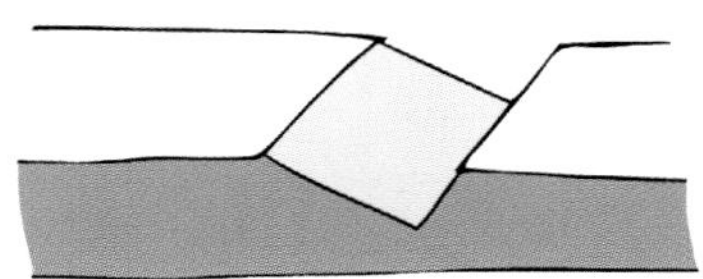

The walls of the channel indicate that the file is twisting to the left as it is pushed through the channel. To correct, roll the wrist slightly toward the right and focus on the right-angled edge of the file, cutting an even, V-shaped channel.

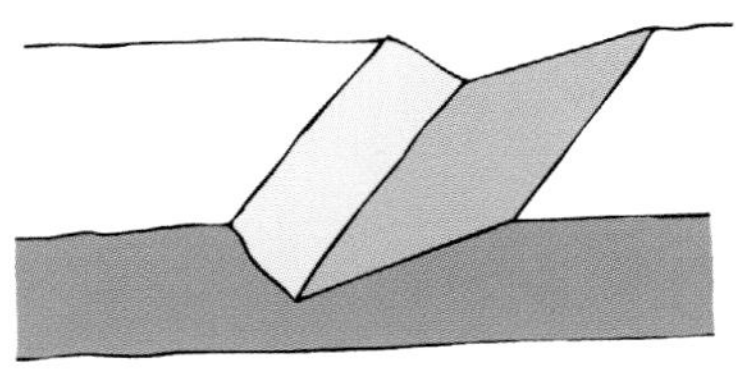

The walls of the channel indicate that the file is twisting to the right as it is pushed through the channel. To correct, roll the wrist slightly toward the left and focus on the right-angled edge of the file, cutting an even, V-shaped channel.

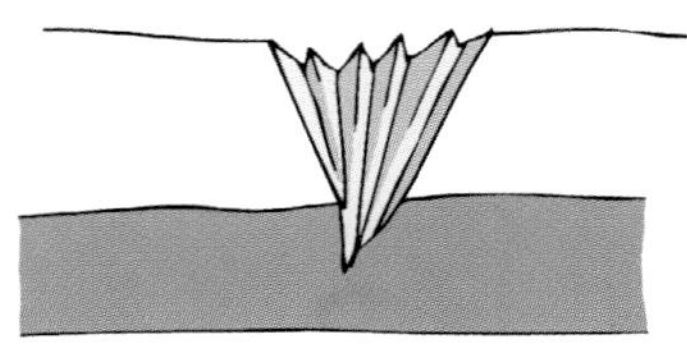

When the walls of the channel resemble the River Nile Estuary, this indicates that a downhill filing action has been applied whilst the wrist pivots and twists from left to right. To correct, drop and steady the wrist and focus on pushing the right-angled edge of the file evenly through the base of the channel.

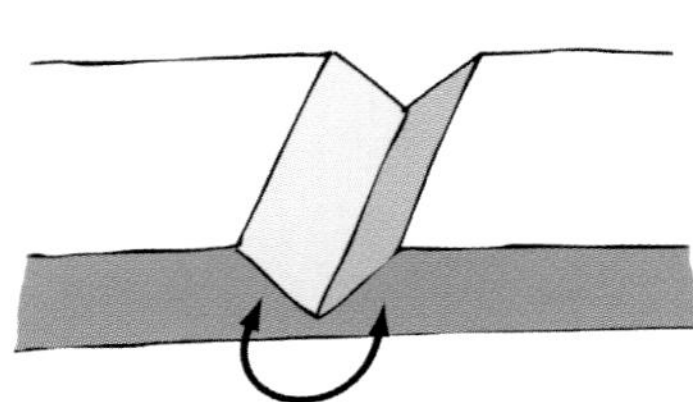

This diagram shows a perfect channel. The walls are evenly cut and the cross section is a well-balanced V-shape.

conical, fancy-shaped mounts

A reasonable selection of ready-made, fancy-shaped conical mounts are available from the larger bullion and tool suppliers, and it is always worth taking a look to see what is out there before embarking on the journey of construction. As outlined in the previous chapter, the beauty of a ready-made mount is that, because they are cast, they are free from solder seams. If the shape of mount you need is not available to buy, then invest in a steel collet block and former, and use it to adapt a round mount to the shape required.

It is also worth mentioning here that chenier is also ideal material to reshape. Seam-free, it will withstand the force required to morph it into another shape.

Having said that, it is still important to know how to construct a fancy-shaped conical mount, so for the next example we will see how a constructed round conical mount can be made square using a square collet block and former. Then a little later we will take a look at the seating and setting processes.

In this example the dimension of the square stone is 5mm x 5mm, and the final mount will be as bearer four described on p.18. The stone is required to sit on top of its mount before seating so the metal strip needs to be 0.8mm thick. It is important to note that during reshaping the dimensions of the mount will be reduced by 1mm, so to account for this we must start by constructing a round conical mount to fit a 6mm diameter stone.

RESHAPING A ROUND CONICAL MOUNT

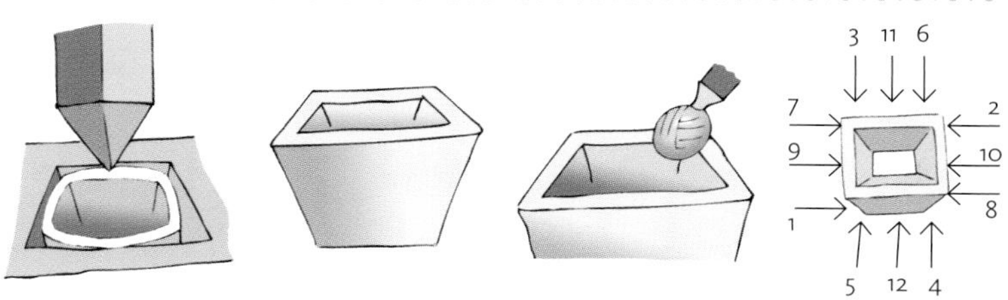

▶ Using the template in Chapter 2 (p.29), plot a round conical mount for a 6mm diameter stone on sheet metal 0.8mm thick.

▶ Pierce out the plotted 'arc'. Anneal, cool and pickle. Use a pair of snipe-nosed pliers to curl the 'arced' strip into a cone. Bring the ends together in a good join and solder the seam with hard solder. Pickle.

▶ True the mount. Place the mount in an appropriate-sized recess of a round collet block. Insert the male former and true the shape by tapping the former with a hide mallet. Once true, anneal gently, cool and pickle.

▶ Reshape the mount from round to square. Place the round mount into a large recess of a square collet block. To ensure the solder join does not tear, position the seam in the middle of one of the collet sides. Insert the square male former and tap gently with a hide mallet to collapse the mount into a soft square shape. Anneal, cool and pickle. Move the mount into the next smaller recess and tap again. Repeat the process until a well-defined square conical mount has been formed.

▶ Prepare the square mount for setting. Level both the top and bottom of the mount using a hand file, then remove file marks with emery paper.

▶ Seat the stone. Create a bearer ledge to seat the girdle of the stone using a stone-setting burr. Start burring in the centre of one side, carefully working the burr into each corner. Burring should stop when the bearer is positioned at its 'optimum' depth (see p.18). True and define the bearer using a knife-edge scorper.

▶ Setting the stone. Once the stone is seated, a 'rub-over'-style setting is carried out to secure it in place.

4. rub-over

Louise O'Neill, Set of six stacking rings. Round and marquise-cut tourmalines set in 18ct white gold. Photo: FXP Photography.

The rub-over setting is the oldest and most basic form of setting, with examples found dating back to ancient times.

Due to its relatively uncomplicated nature, the rub-over or bezel setting is usually the first form of setting taught to jewellery students and apprentices alike, and it is often at this early stage that a student develops either a love or a loathing for working with stones.

so how does it work?

This type of setting provides the stone with a greater protection from scratches, knocks and general wear and tear, because the girdle of the stone is completely enclosed by a wall of metal. This wall is known as the bezel. During the setting process the bezel is 'rubbed down', using a setting tool onto the girdle of the stone, to secure it in place. A rub-over setting can also go by the name of a bezel setting.

Contemporary developments of the rub-over setting have shown that it is not always necessary for the bezel to completely enclose a stone's girdle. For years jewellery designers and manufacturers have been experimenting with this concept, and collectively they have succeeded in creating many variations on the theme. A half bezel or segmented bezel can give a mount a less bulky feel and enhance and emphasize the beauty of a stone by creating a lighter and more elegant design.

Chapter 2, Mounts and the Principles of Setting, describes in detail the processes involved in the construction and setting techniques for straight-sided and conical mounts, both of which in fact are a basic form of the rub-over style of setting. To repeat it all again would be an unnecessary task. So for this section of the book we are going to 'step outside the box' and show how the construction methods for a basic rub-over mount can be adapted into something a little more exciting – to push one's personal boundaries can be a challenge but is often very rewarding.

the example

Of the two rings pictured here the one set with the marquise black onyx cabochon has been chosen for this example. The following step-by-step guide and accompanying CAD illustrations are designed to outline the processes behind constructing and setting a mount of this design.

TOOLS AND MATERIALS USED

- Marquise black onyx cabochon stone 12mm x 6mm
- 18ct yellow gold disc 0.8mm thick with a diameter of 14mm.
- Doming block and punches
- Piercing blade and frame
- Hard 18ct yellow gold solder
- 2-cut hand file
- Emery stick
- A selection of ball burrs
- Pendant motor
- Flat scorper
- Flat square-section push stick
- Safety back file

Sonia Cheadle, black onyx cocktail rings.
18ct yellow gold and black onyx cabochon stones.
Photo: Robert Holmes.

the mount

First the dimensions of the stone have to be taken. Traditionally, a marquise is cut with a length that equals twice the diameter. For the example here the length, measured tip to tip, is 12mm, so the diameter, measured side to side, will be 6mm.

The mount in this example is made from an 18ct yellow-gold disc of metal with a thickness of 0.8mm. When constructing a mount of this design it is the length of the stone that is the key measurement, because the length of the marquise will dictate the diameter of the disc required.

For this example a disc with a diameter 14mm will be sufficient to create a mount for a marquise with a length of 12mm. The 2mm difference allows for thickness of metal, as well as metal loss, during the construction process. Once this is decided the construction process can begin.

- ▶ Using a pair of dividers a circle with a diameter of 14mm is scribed onto the surface of the 18ct yellow-gold sheet. Using a piercing frame the circle is then cut out.
- ▶ A hand file is used to true the circle round, and all file marks are removed with emery paper.
- ▶ The disc is then annealed, cooled and pickled.
- ▶ Next place the disc into a recess of a steel doming block, selecting the one that best echoes the curve of the marquise.
- ▶ With the disc in situ the appropriate-sized doming punch is placed over the disc and tapped with a hide mallet. This action in turn extrudes the disc into a dome shape.
- ▶ The rim of the dome is filed flat with a hand file, and all file marks are then removed using an emery stick.
- ▶ The dome is then pierced, straight down the middle. To create the marquise shape the two halves of the dome are brought together rim to rim, and the seam is then soldered with 18ct yellow-gold hard solder.

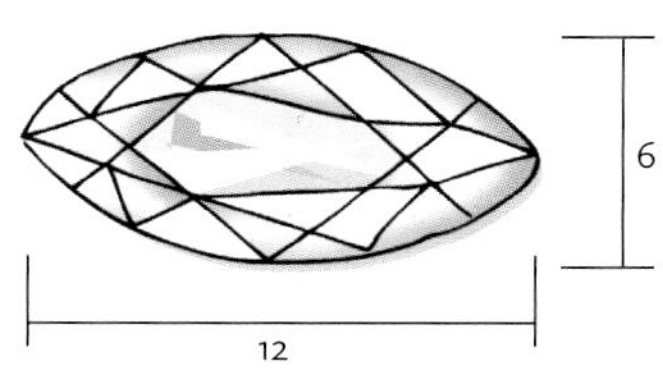

Marquise dimensions.

Marquise stone in doming recess.

Doming.

The dome cut into two halves.

- The opening of the mount is filed level then smoothed with emery paper.
- The mount is now complete and soldered to the ring shank, ready for the bearer to be positioned.
- A ball burr is used to create the bearer and is worked carefully into the corners of the marquise shape. The bearer should be positioned so that the marquise stone sits below the surface and at optimum depth for the curve of its domed top.
- A flat scorper is used to true and define the bearer by hand, until the stone sits level.
- With the stone seated, the rub-over can now be performed.

Two halves to make a whole.

the setting

When a marquise-shaped stone is set in the rub-over style, the same principles apply as when setting a round stone. Each push of the setting tool must be applied from opposing sides. Great care should be taken, however, when turning down the corners of a marquise. Work slowly around the mount, easing the metal gently down onto the stone. If you turn down the corners of the mount too abruptly they may 'peak': it will then be impossible to turn the metal down in these areas and the pressure from trying may cause the stone to break.

Bearer ledge being burred.

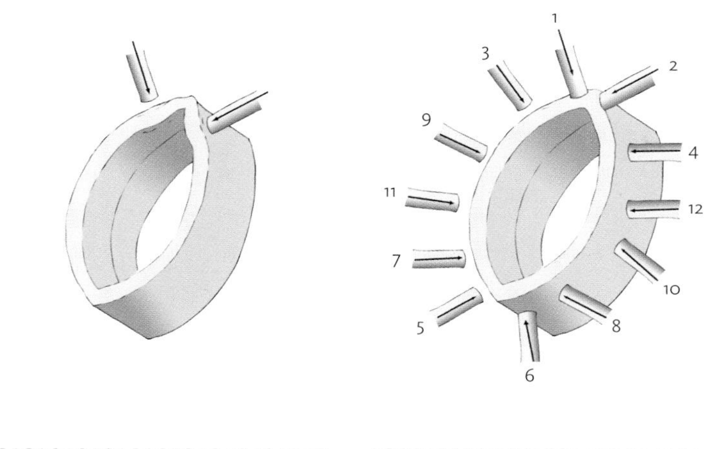

Peaked corner.

Suggested 'push' order.

Work around the rim of the mount a couple of times to smooth out any lumps and bumps and ensure the stone is locked in place. A quick file and final emery will erase any visible setting marks, though care must be taken not to scratch the stone.

5. claw

Cox & Power, Mandarin Ring. 18ct rose gold, mandarin garnet and diamond. Photo: Tim Kent.

The claw style of setting became popular in the early 1800s and is often associated with more traditional styles of jewellery. The diamond solitaire ring, which is claw-set, has to be one of the most successful and famous items of jewellery ever designed. In 1961, the film adaptation of Truman Capote's novel Breakfast at Tiffany's led to a marked increase in demand for the Tiffany diamond solitaire as thousands flocked to the famous department store wanting to buy a piece of Hepburn romance and glamour. Fifty years on and demand is still high. In every high street in every city you will find a thousand adaptations of the same ring. So, whoever said romance was dead was clearly wrong. It very much alive, but perhaps a little predictable.

so how does it work?

Traditionally, the claw style of setting comprises between four and six claws arranged around the girdle of the stone. The claws are pushed over and burnished down on top of the crown of the stone to secure it. This style of setting is usually used for transparent, faceted stones. As there is no metal directly under the stone and the sides of the mount are open, light floods in and around the area, brightening the reflection of light and enhancing the refractory qualities of the exposed stone.

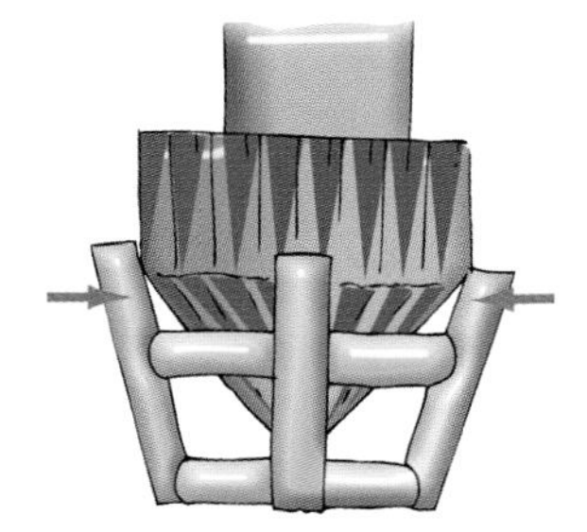

Wire claw mount and stone-setting burr.

the mount

Traditionally, a mount for this style of setting is either constructed from wire or is formed by cutting sections from the wall of a conical-shaped mount. The bearer is often formed from a thin wire collet soldered between the claws; in a more contemporary version, however, it is formed by cutting directly into the claws. There are various ways to cut the bearer to the required shape, but the easiest and most common method is to use a steel burr and pendant motor.

When seating a stone in a wire collet, a straight-sided stone-setting burr is used, with a diameter to match that of the girdle. The straight edge opens out the claws to the exact diameter of the stone, and the tip of the burr removes metal from inside the collet, allowing the pavilion to be seated. When creating the bearer directly into the claws, a small bearing-cutter burr, matching the size of the girdle, is used to undercut each claw to form the seat for the girdle of the stone.

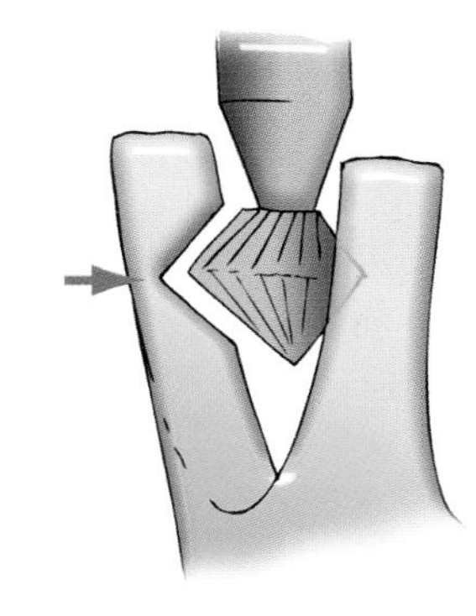

Cut claw mount and bearing-cutter burr.

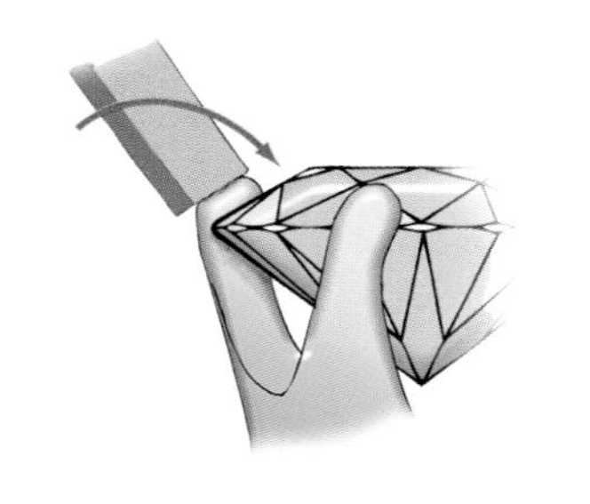

Claw being set.

Once the stone is seated the setting process can begin.

The construction process of a claw mount involves multiple solder joins. To achieve this alone demands a high level of technical ability executed with extreme precision and skill. It would be fair to say that perfecting this form of construction takes years of practice.

Help is at hand, however, and a wide variety of ready-made claw mounts can be bought from the larger bullion and tool suppliers. The ready-mades are designed to fit only the simpler, standard sizes and shapes of stone, but on the plus side they are made using the casting process, which means there are no vulnerable solder joins.

the setting

Once the stone is seated, whether in a ready-made or a handmade mount, the claws are pushed over onto the crown to secure the stone in place. A flat, square-ended pusher is used to carry out the setting process, and the claws are then rounded with a file to eliminate sharp edges. After gentle emerying, taking care not to scratch the stone, the final polish can be applied.

the example

Chrysoprase ring.

Here we are going to look at the processes involved in constructing a contemporary 18ct yellow-gold, thick claw mount for a 10mm round chrysoprase cabochon stone. To be a little more creative, the bearer for the girdle of the cabochon will be cut directly into the claws and the stone will be seated upside down within the mount. Because the stone is set directly into the claws it is essential that a substantial thickness of wire is used so as to prevent the claws from rocking and being pushed apart. Round-section wire with a diameter of 1.8mm has been chosen for this example.

As with all other styles of setting, the diameter and depth of stone must be measured before construction can begin. In this case, however, because the cabochon is seated upside down and the claws come from underneath the stone, the depth of the stone is what is crucial here.

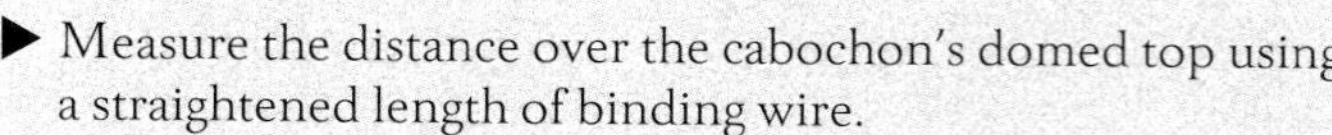

▶ Measure the distance over the cabochon's domed top using a straightened length of binding wire.

- Multiply this distance by two and add an extra 4mm, to allow for metal loss during construction. This will give you the total length of gold wire required.
- Cut the gold wire into two equal lengths. Anneal, cool and pickle.
- Using a pair of half-round pliers, ease each section of wire into an arc shape.
- Check the shape of each arc against the stone for both diameter and depth. The curve of the arc needs to follow the dome of the cabochon, and the girdle of the stone needs to rest equally on all four claws, covering approximately one third of each.
- Once these two factors are decided, each arc is tapped true on a steel triblet using a hide mallet.
- Next, a round needle file is used to file a small groove, dead centre, on the inside of one of the arcs. The process is repeated for the second arc, though this time the groove is filed on the outside.
- The grooved arcs are then slotted together at 90°, one inside the other, to form the four claws of the mount.
- Then, the two arcs are assembled on a heatproof block and are soldered together using 18ct yellow hard gold solder.
- Now that the mount is complete it can be fitted to the ring shank, and the bearer for the girdle can be cut.
- For greater stability when set, the stone in this example needs to be seated as low as possible in the mount. This depth is best assessed by eye. A pair of dividers is then used to mark the inside of each claw identically where the bearer is to be cut.
- Using a bearing-cutter burr, this mark is then opened out to accept the girdle of the stone.
- The stone is then seated in the bearer and the claws are pushed over and rubbed down onto the stone, securing it in place.
- With the stone now set, the ring gets one last file and emery before the final polish is applied.

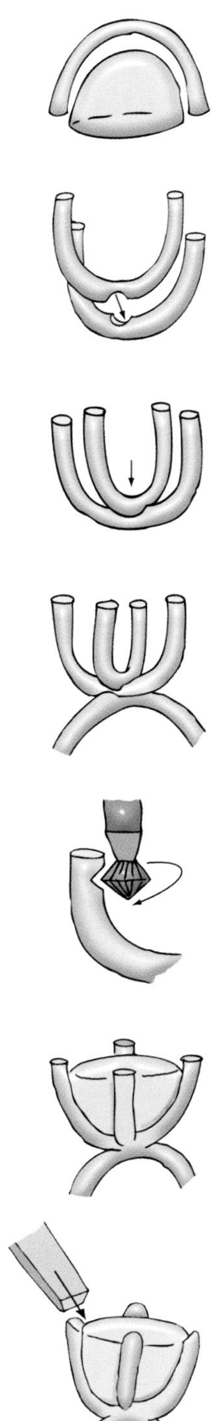

6. gypsy

Malcolm Betts, gypsy-set bangle. 22ct yellow gold, diamond and ruby. Photo: Graham Rae.

In the UK this style of setting is, inexplicably, referred to as a gypsy setting. Disappointingly, research to try to uncover the origin of this term revealed no definite evidence as to its true origin, though a tenuous link to Gypsy Rose Lee caused great amusement. In other countries the terms 'flush setting' or 'burnished setting' are used, which, although not terribly imaginative, are both more accurate descriptions of the setting style.

First introduced several decades ago, the gypsy setting is traditionally used to set small round faceted stones. With no visible evidence of any setting techniques – whether a claw, grain or rub-over – the gypsy setting allows a random, almost whimsical scattering of stones across the surface of the metal.

A gypsy setting is a great way to add sparkle to the simplest items of jewellery without any major expense.

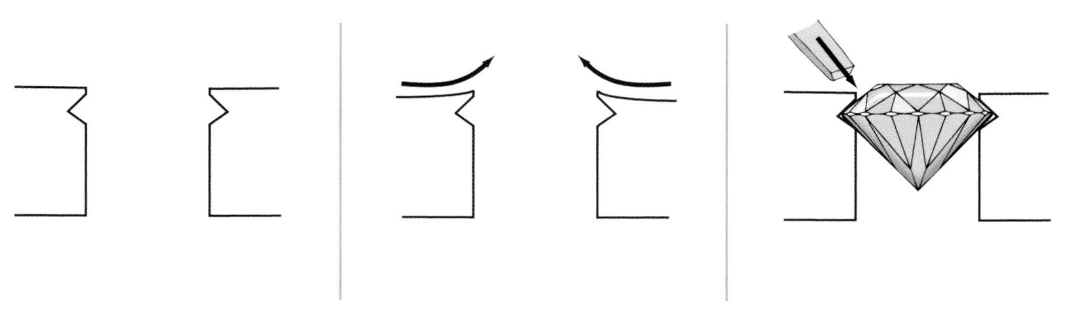

How a gypsy setting works.

so how does it work?

A gypsy setting is a variation of the rub-over style of setting because metal from around the seated stone is pushed down onto the girdle to secure it. The variation is the way in which the seat for the stone is created. In a traditional gypsy setting a small 'bearing-cutter' steel burr is used to undercut the inner wall of the mount. In addition to creating a seat, this action creates a small lip of metal around the top of the hole. To allow the stone into its seat this lip has to be teased upwards. The stone is then dropped into position and the lip is pushed back down and onto the girdle of the stone, thus securing it in place.

the mount

With the gypsy style of setting there is no separately formed mount. Instead, drilling a hole directly into the surface of the jewellery item creates the mount. Because of this, gypsy setting is best suited to small round faceted stones set into a flat surface.

Curved surfaces can be gypsy-set, but for this to be successful, stones with a small diameter need to be used; and the tighter the curve, the smaller the diameter of the stone needs to be. To help clarify this point, visualise the girdle of the stone as a solid plane sitting completely below the surface of the metal. Attempting to gypsy-set a large stone into a curved surface would be like trying to set a dinner plate into a beach ball.

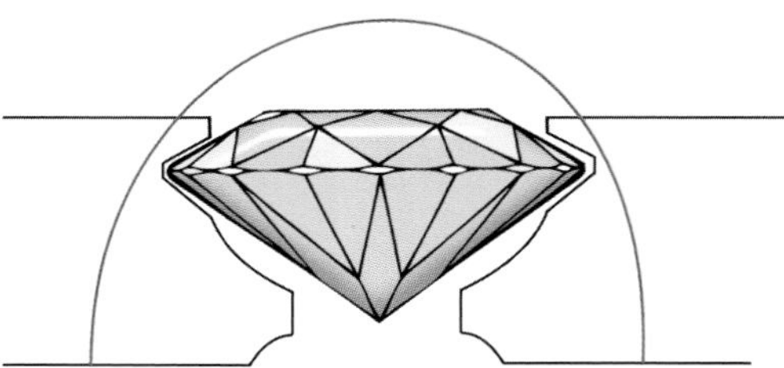

Gypsy setting in a curved surface.

The image above shows a cross section of a round faceted stone seated in a flat surface. The red arc indicates the cross section of a curved surface. Notice how the majority of the curve would need to be removed in order to seat a stone of this size.

From the earliest stages in the design process, therefore, two considerations must be taken into account:

- The curve of a surface will indicate the optimum diameter of the stone, as the stone needs to be completely embedded in the surface of metal.
- The depth of the stone determines the metal thickness required for the setting to be successful.

When the design is finalised and the item of jewellery has been constructed, the mounting process can begin. The first job here is to drill a pilot hole where each stone is to be located.

The next task is open out the pilot hole to mirror the shape of the stone, while remembering that the hole must remain a fraction smaller than the dimensions of the stone. To do this, choose a stone-setting burr for a round stone, and either a small ball burr or a graver for a fancy-shaped stone.

Once the pilot hole has been opened out, the bearer is then undercut on the inside of the hole. Not only must the bearer be crisp and precise, it also needs to be positioned at the correct depth for the girdle to be secure. This optimum depth can be gauged by assessing the distance from the girdle of the stone to the top of its crown. Optimum depth is shown in the diagram below, marked by a broken red line.

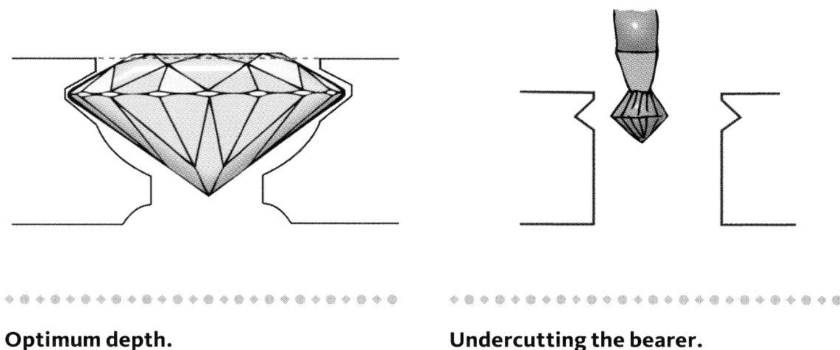

Optimum depth. **Undercutting the bearer.**

When this distance has been established, the bearer is cut using a small bearing-cutter burr and pendant motor. The process of undercutting the bearer creates a small lip of metal around the top of the hole. Using the tip of a burnisher, the lip is then raised to allow the stone to be 'clicked' into its seat.

Seating the stone is the most difficult aspect of this style of setting, as it demands both a high level of concentration and good tool control. Mastering the steps above will take time, practice and repetition. Once this has been achieved, however, the actual setting process will seem relatively simple by comparison – and something to look forward to.

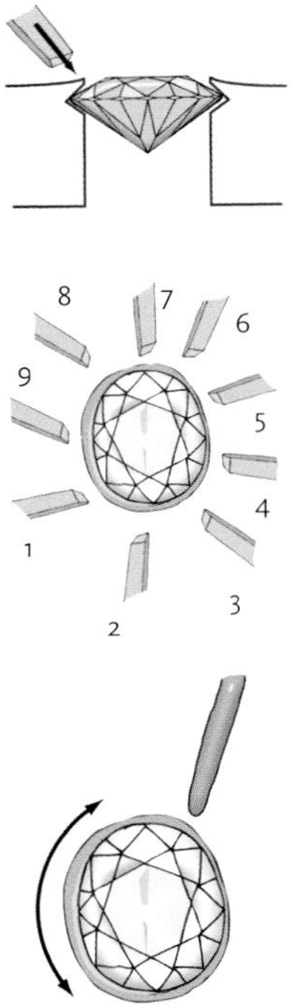

the setting

When the stone is seated and the piece has been secured in either a ring clamp or a setting stick, the setting process can begin.

For this procedure, a flat, square-section pusher is used. The pusher is introduced to the lip of the hole and a slight pressure is applied to push the metal forward and down toward the girdle of the stone. The pusher is worked slowly around the hole whilst the setting stick is rotated, and after a few complete revolutions the lip will be down and the stone locked in its seat. When this is achieved, a pointed burnisher is used to true up, tighten and brighten the inside edge.

The setting is now complete, though it is always advisable at this stage to make absolutely sure that the stone is secure. A quick session in an ultrasonic cleaner will soon reveal the answer. But if the stone is one that is affected by the machine's waves, a careful push of the pavilion through the hole on the reverse of the piece will be just as effective. If the stones break free, the above steps will need to be repeated.

8 7 6 9 5 4 1 3 2

Traditional gypsy-style of setting.

the example

As with many other setting styles, gypsy-setting a round stone is easier than tackling any other shape, because a round hole is what is produced when a drill or burr are used. The real challenge arises when attempting to gypsy-set the fancier-shaped stones. Therefore, for this example we are going to take a look at the processes involved in gypsy-setting a faceted pear, as in the picture on p.58. Besides this, you will find a more detailed look at a 'quick gypsy' solution in Chapter 12, Specialist Tools and Techniques.

The processes outlined below may seem rather complicated, especially for someone who is relatively new to jewellery making, but sometimes it pays to challenge and push ourselves because very little is gained if we always choose the easy option.

so how is it done?

For this bangle, the first job is to decide on a collection of stones and to accurately measure and record the diameter and depth of each one. These measurements are then used to calculate the dimensions of the bangle. The stone with the largest diameter will suggest an appropriate width for the bangle, and the stone that has the greatest depth will indicate the thickness of metal required.

Once this has been decided the exact amount of 22ct gold can be bought and the bangle can be made. 22ct yellow gold has a soft and malleable quality, which makes gypsy-setting fancy-cut stones an awful lot easier.

For the purpose of this exercise, and to help explain the processes involved in gypsy-setting a fancy-cut stone, the pear-shaped diamond in the centre of the image on p.58 has been chosen as the example.

- ▶ With construction of the bangle complete, the next step would be to drill a pilot hole, smaller than the diameter of the stone, in the position where the stone is to be set.
- ▶ The pilot hole is then opened out to mirror the shape of the pear, remembering that the hole must remain a fraction smaller than the dimensions of the stone.
- ▶ This process is best done in two parts. First a large ball burr is used to remove metal to form the round section of the shape, and a smaller ball burr is chosen to extend the recess into a triangle.
- ▶ Then a flat scorper is used to cut and define the pear-shaped recess by hand.
- ▶ The tip of the pear shape is the most delicate and vulnerable part of the stone, so any metal directly under the tip on the inside of the hole needs to be removed. A tiny ball burr is used to do this action, which in turn will divert any pressure away from this vulnerable area, helping to keep the tip intact.
- ▶ Now the inside of the hole can be undercut to create the seat for the girdle, using a bearing-cutter burr.
- ▶ With the seat in place the lip of the hole is gently lifted and the stone is popped into position. With a pear shape, the tip of the stone must always go in first.
- ▶ The rim can now be pushed back down onto the stone and eased toward the girdle using a flat square-section pusher.
- ▶ Finally, a pointed burnisher is used around the whole of the setting to true the edge and tighten the setting.
- ▶ The setting is now complete.

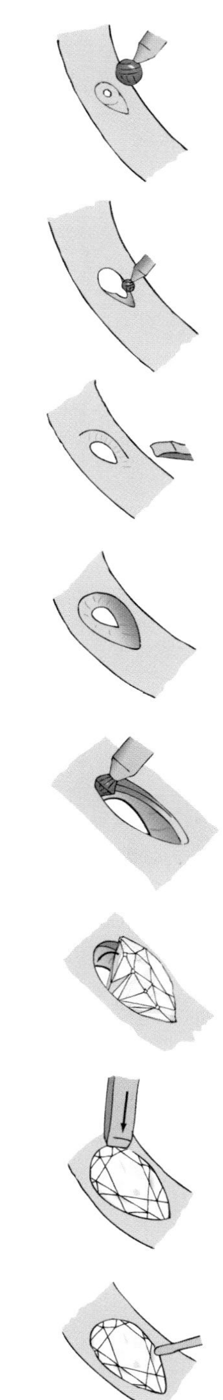

How to construct a gypsy setting for a fancy-cut stone.

7. pavé

Shaun Leane, 18ct white gold, tsavorite and white diamond Tribal Deco earrings.
18-ct white gold, pavé-set tsavorite, diamond and onyx beads. Photo: Shaun Leane.

The pavé style of setting has to be one of the most difficult to achieve. Throughout the whole process accuracy is paramount, and with the stones in such close proximity there really is very little room for error. The techniques involved require a completely different set of specialist skills that take commitment and dedication to acquire and months of practice to fine-tune and finally master. This, unfortunately, cannot be delivered in a single chapter; to cover the topic thoroughly would require another book. The purpose of this chapter, therefore, is to explain the principles of mount design, construction and preparation in the pavé style and to outline the setting process.

The French word pavé translates as 'paved', and the pavé style of setting consists of a tight interlocking group of identically sized stones, set across a flat or convex surface. Pavé is primarily used to set small round faceted stones and is often linked with more traditional jewellery designs. When executed professionally, the finished pavé creates a clean and elegant flow of gemstones that sweep across the metal, transforming the surface into an uninterrupted sea of sparkle.

Traditionally associated with diamond houses such as Cartier, Tiffany and Van Cleef & Arpels in the early 1900s, the pavé style has recently returned to the forefront of contemporary jewellery, with designers such as JAR, Stephen Webster and Shaun Leane giving a new lease of life to this time-honoured technique.

so how does it work?

Pavé can be seen as a hybrid of both the gypsy and the claw styles of setting – the gypsy because the stones are completely embedded in the surface of the metal, and the claw because during the setting process slivers of metal are raised around the hole and pushed over onto the girdle of the stone to secure it in its seat, each sliver acting as a tiny claw before the final graining process takes place.

the mount

The stones are mounted directly into the surface of the metal, either row upon row in a square-grid formation or offset to create a honeycomb effect.

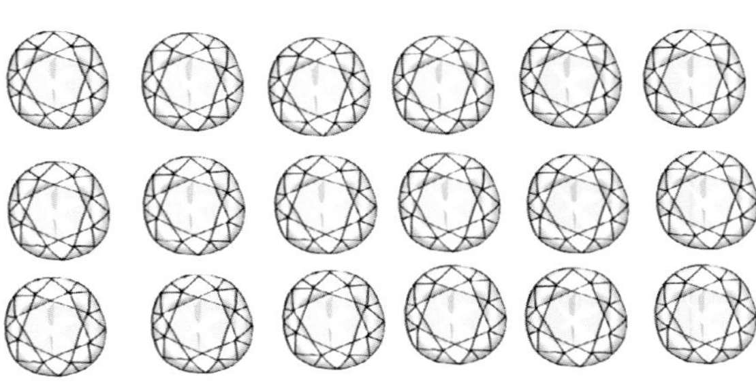

Square-grid pavé formation.

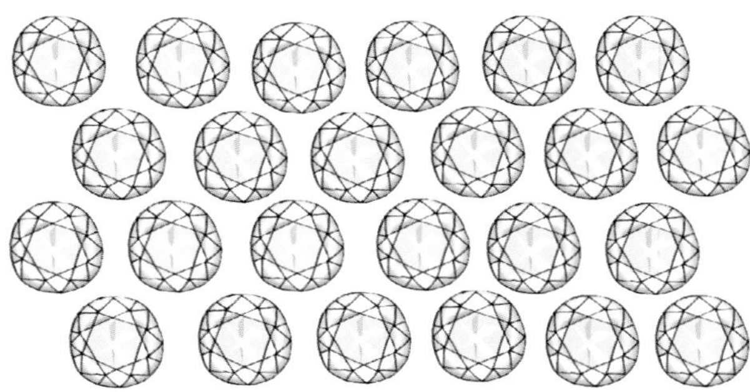

Honeycomb pavé formation.

The first task is to determine which of the two mount formations best suits the jewellery design and the size of the stones being used. An outline of the desired setting area is scribed onto the surface of the piece, then the surface of the metal is made tacky by dabbing it all over with a wax peg. The stones are then tacked in place, table down, to check positioning and to calculate the number of stones required per row.

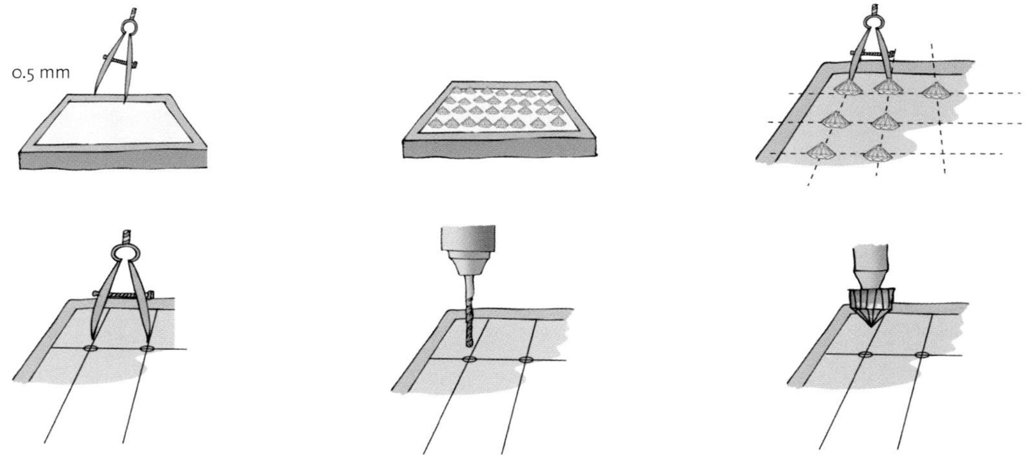

0.5 mm

How to construct a pavé setting.

With the stones tacked in place a pair of dividers is used to measure the distance between two culets of neighbouring stones, and a second pair of dividers is opened out to find the centre line of each row.

With these two measurements set, the stones are cleared from the metal and the dividers are used to plot and score the position of each stone onto the surface of the metal. The centre line of each row is scribed first using the measurement recorded with the second set of dividers. These lines are then divided, using the first set of dividers, to indicate the position of each culet and to pinpoint the exact spot where a pilot hole needs to be drilled. With the positions of the stones located, the piece is mounted onto a setting stick and the pilot holes are drilled.

Next, each pilot hole is opened out to create the bearer, using a stone-setting burr with a diameter to match the stone's girdle. The bearer is positioned so that the girdle of the stone is completely below the surface of the metal, with only a sliver of table seen when viewed across the horizon. Once all bearers are in place and the stones are seated, the setting process can begin.

the setting

In either layout, whether square-grid or honeycomb, the stones are initially fastened in place by raised slivers of metal positioned equidistantly between the stones. This process is known as 'raising the grains', and is achieved using a half-round scorper. Raising grains is a very intricate procedure, and it is essential that the placement and movement of the scorper are executed with absolute precision.

For a single row of pavé the order in which the grains are raised is similar to the pushing order of a rub-over-style setting, whereby every move is executed from opposite sides of the stone.

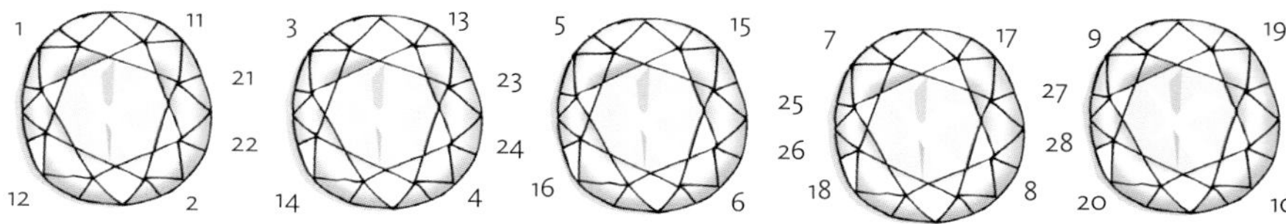

Order for raising the grains in a single pavé row.

For a cluster of pavé the grain order is best viewed as three circles: outer, inner and centre.

The grains of the outer circle are raised first, followed by those positioned around the inner circle, and finally the grains around the centre circle are raised. The larger the cluster the more concentric circles of grains there will be.

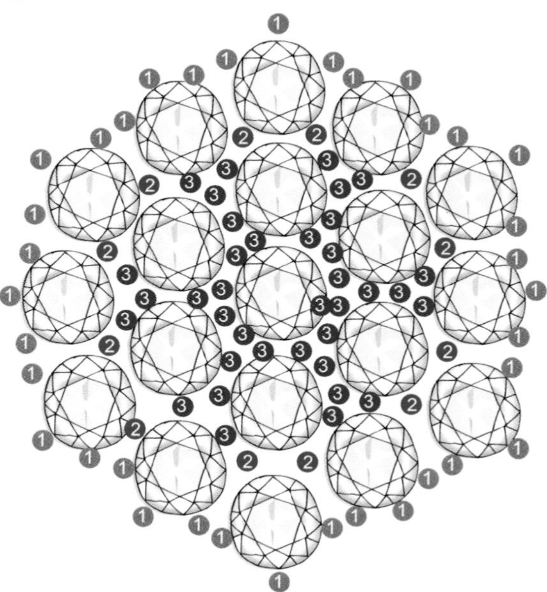

Order for raising the grains in a pavé cluster.

When all the stones are securely tacked in place, any excess metal between the grains is removed using a knife-edge scorper. Once this process is complete the grains are then rounded off and burnished using a hollow graining tool. The setting is now complete and can be removed from the setting stick.

the example

This example looks in detail at the process involved in making a pavé-set diamond bangle using the 'lost wax' casting technique, a technique which plays an important role in the small jewellery studio.

The pavé-set diamond bangle pictured below is cast in 18ct white gold, around which 118 round-brilliant-cut diamonds have been pavé-set.

The lost-wax technique was chosen as the method of construction for two reasons. Firstly, the finished bangle will be free of solder joins. Secondly, casting is more cost effective than fabricating each bangle individually when you take into account the time taken to drill 118 holes, plus the cost of metal wastage, a direct by-product of drilling.

Sonia Cheadle, Ring of Fire Bangle.
18ct white gold and pavé-set diamond.
Photo: Matt Lee.

The first process in the lost-wax technique is to make a master of the item to be cast. Making a master bangle means the task of positioning and drilling 118 holes need only be performed once, as every bangle then produced from the master mould will be identical and exact. By utilizing the lost-wax technique we are in effect creating our own ready-made mount, which saves time and, consequently, money.

Brilliant, I hear you say. However, there is one slight downside with using the lost-wax technique, and that is the matter of shrinkage. In brief, an item cast from a master mould can be up to 15% smaller than the master itself. If this is not taken into account when constructing a master, the end result will be a ready-made mount that is too small for the intended stones. To counteract this shrinkage, therefore, we need to make the master a little bigger than the final item required. Unfortunately, there is no exact science for calculating the right amount of shrinkage.

The following series of images is intended to outline the lost-wax technique, clarify the process involved, and help form a greater understanding of how it can be used within a small jewellery studio.

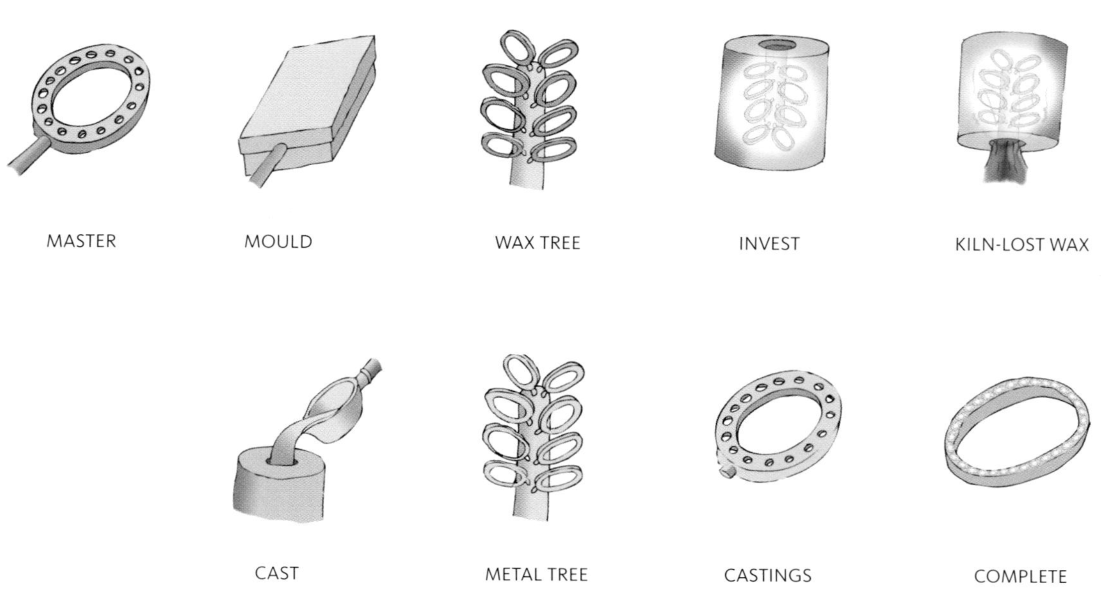

The lost-wax method of casting.

so where do you start when making a master?

To help answer this question we need an example. Let's take a look at how the master was produced for the Ring of Fire diamond bangle pictured on p.69.

The dimensions of the master were extrapolated from the dimensions of the finished bangle, which in turn were dictated by the diameter and depth of the stones being set. The diamonds are 1.5mm in diameter with an average depth of 0.9mm. Therefore, to accommodate pavé-set diamonds this size the final bangle needs to be 2mm square. So to account for shrinkage, the master bangle was made from 2.3mm-square silver wire.

When construction of the master bangle was complete the next task was to plot the position of each individual stone.

A pair of dividers, opened to half the diameter of the square-section wire, was used to scribe the centre line around the face of the bangle. Next the centre line needed to be divided to show the location of each stone. It is important to note here that the holes would also shrink during the casting process. So to account for this, cubic zirconia with a diameter of 1.8mm were used to plot the location of the stones.

The face of the master bangle was made tacky and the 1.8mm cubic zirconia were laid out, table down, all around the circumference. Once the stones were in place, a pair of dividers was used to measure and record the distance between the culet of neighbouring stones. With this measurement set, the stones were cleared from the face and the centre line was divided to pinpoint the position of every stone. When the surface of the master bangle had been correctly marked up, the pilot holes were drilled using a 1.3mm drill. The master was now complete.

At this stage, due to the processes and machinery involved in the lost-wax technique, the master is usually sent to a professional casting foundry. The next time you see your item it will be a cast version of the master – perfectly proportioned with the pilot holes already in place – and after a quick file and emery the setting processes can begin.

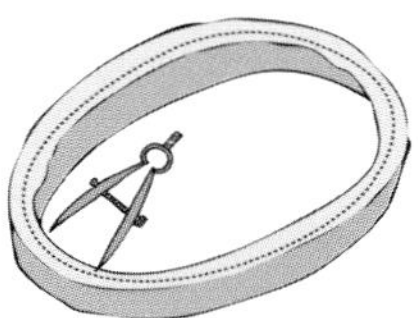

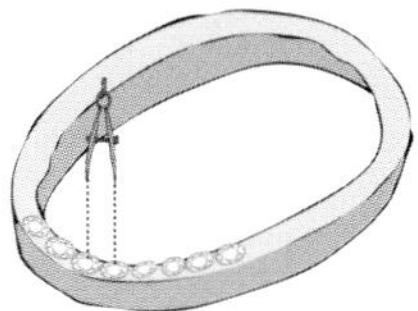

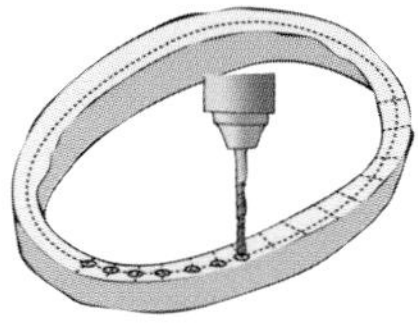

Plotting the position of the stones.

8. channel

Sonia Cheadle, Platinum ring. Channel-set diamond. Photo: Robert Holmes.

Channel setting is a term commonly used to describe a row of stones aligned in a channel side by side with their girdles touching so that no metal is visible between them. The restraining walls run parallel on either side of the stones so that the stones appear to be suspended within the channel.

This style of setting is extremely popular these days in the design of wedding bands and commitment rings, where a complete circle of stones set within a channel is often used to symbolize eternal love. As well as the classic eternity ring this style of setting can also be found sweeping the shoulders of a more traditionally designed engagement ring or a fabulously flamboyant cocktail ring.

The level of skill required to successfully achieve either style is on a par with that of the pavé, as once again accuracy and precision are paramount throughout every stage.

so how does it work?

The channel style of setting can be viewed as a cross between the gypsy and the rub-over. It is like the gypsy because the stones sit on a bearer below the surface of the metal; it is like the rub-over because, once seated, the wall of the mount is pushed over onto the girdle of the stones to secure them in place. The main difference is that in channel setting all the stones are nestled together in one elongated mount as opposed to being isolated.

There are two ways to create this style of setting. Deciding which one to use depends on the shape of the stones being set, as one style is suited to round faceted stones while the other is better suited to either square or baguette. Both styles use the same method of construction, whereby a channel must be created, but the difference between the two is cleverly concealed on the inside of the mount and involves the process of positioning and cutting the bearer.

Given that both styles of channel setting use the same method of construction, let us start by taking a look at how a channel is created, after which we can look at the processes involved in seating round, square and baguette-cut stones.

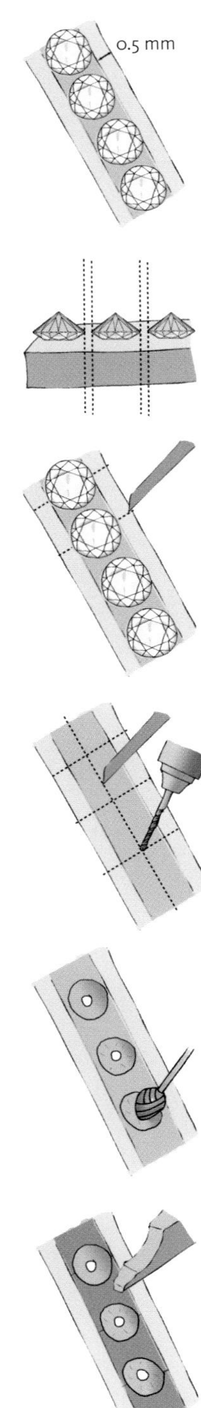

the channel mount

A selection of burrs, scorpers and files are used to create the channel by removing metal from within a specified area. The first task, in which the diameter and depth of the stones play an important role, is to plot this area.

The diameter of the stones dictates the width of the channel, and the stone with the greatest depth will indicate the thickness of metal required for the stones to be secure and the setting process a success. It is essential even at this early stage that extreme precision is exercised to avoid cutting a channel too wide or too deep, errors that would render the mount unusable.

The techniques involved at this stage of the process are the same regardless of the shape of the stones being set. So, for the purpose of this exercise, the following guide and accompanying illustrations outline the processes involved in creating a channelled mount for 2mm round faceted stones.

- Using a pair of dividers the borders of the channel are plotted onto the surface of the piece. An ideal width would be when the girdles of the stones rest on top of the channel and cover approximately one-third of the surrounding scribed border. The border itself needs to be at least 0.5mm wide. The centre line is then scribed down.

- Next the surface of the piece is made tacky and the stones are laid out in channel formation. A slight gap needs to be left between each stone, otherwise the girdles of the stones may overlap once inside the channel.

- Whilst in the layout position the centre of each stone is marked on each side of the channel using a fine-pointed scriber. The stones are then cleared from the surface and the marks for each stone are joined through the centre line.

- The point where each vertical line crosses the centre line is marked with the scriber, and a pilot hole is drilled on the exact spot.

- When all the pilot holes have been drilled, each one is opened out using a bud burr to approximately three quarters of the diameter of the stones being set. So for the example here a bud burr with a diameter of 1.5mm would suffice.

- Now a flat scorper is used to remove the metal between each 'burred' pilot hole to start forming the channel.
- With the basis of a channel now formed the next step is to create the seats for the individual stones, and it is here that the processes have to be adapted to accommodate the different-shaped stones. To maintain continuity we proceed from here with our 2mm round faceted stones as the example, but we'll return to this stage later in the chapter to look at the processes involved in seating square and baguette-cut stones.

seating a channel of 2mm round faceted stones

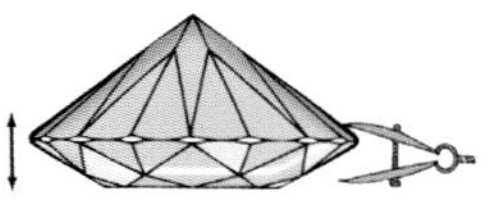

- To create the individual seats each burred pilot hole is 'cut' with a stone-setting burr with a diameter the same as the hole. The purpose of these seats is to support the stones' pavilions once inside the channel, so the required depth of each seat would equal the approximate distance from the top of a stone's table to the bottom of its girdle. A pair of dividers set to this measurement can help monitor depth during this procedure, and the seats are cut for this example using a 1.5mm stone-setting burr.

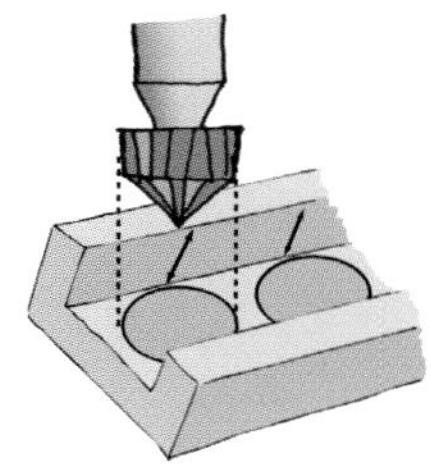

- When all the seats are cut, the walls and basin of the channel can be defined using a flat scorper or square needle file.

- The next process is to undercut one of the channel walls so as to create the bearer for the girdles of the stones. To accomplish this, a bearing-cutter burr is introduced into the channel so that its pavilion runs parallel with the channel basin. In this position the widest part of the bearing-cutter burr is used to cut a groove that runs the full length of the channel. Once the bearer has been cut, the channel is ready to accept the stones.

- To seat the stones in the channel the girdle of each stone is first tilted into the undercut bearer. This action will allow the stone to be gently pushed into its seat. This process is carried out with every stone. Once they are all seated, the setting process can begin.

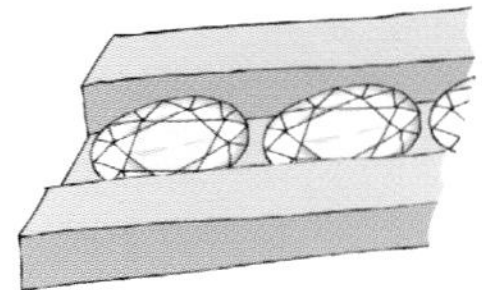

To interrupt the explanation at this critical stage of the process might cause confusion, so, departing from the format of previous chapters, to maintain the flow we will move directly to the final stage of this process – setting the channelled mount of 2mm round faceted stones.

setting a channel of 2mm round faceted stones

- The first task of the setting process is to pre-tighten the sides of the channel using a pair of snipe-nosed pliers.
- Straddling the stones one by one with the pliers, the side of the mount that has not been undercut is brought down and towards the stones' girdles by gentle squeezing.
- Once down, the tightening process is repeated for the opposite side. The purpose of this procedure is to lock the stones into their seats so as to prevent them shifting during the next stage of the setting process.
- With the stones now locked into their seats, the walls of the channel need to be tapped down a little further to ensure the stones are secure. This procedure is done using a flat-ended chasing tool and hammer, and, as before, the side that gets tapped first is the one that has not been undercut.

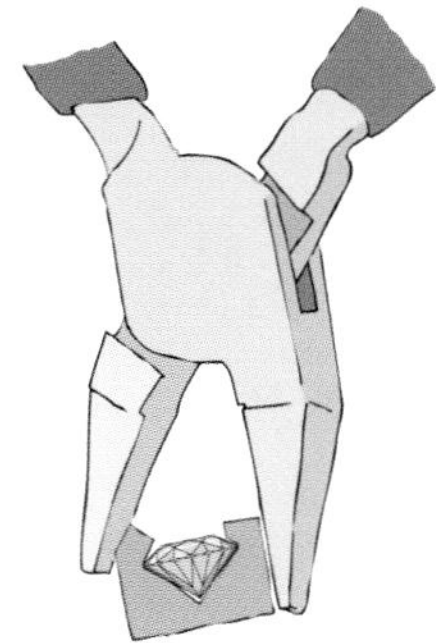

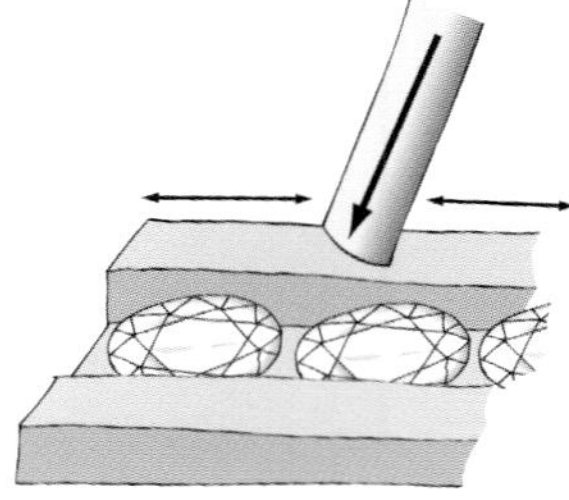

- ▶ With the piece fixed into a setting stick, which is itself secured into a bench vice, the chasing tool is introduced to the wall at one end of the channel and a sweep of gentle 'taps' is chased along its entire length.
- ▶ The process is repeated for the opposite wall. After a couple of clean sweeps along both walls, the stones should be secure, whereupon the setting process is complete.
- ▶ To finish the setting, any hammer marks should be carefully removed using a safety back file, and the walls given a quick, final emery.

By now we should have a greater understanding of how a channel mount is created and how a row of 2mm round faceted stones is seated and set. As mentioned a little earlier in this chapter, the processes involved in seating square or baguette-cut stones differ from the processes outlined above.

Because the 'square drill' is yet to be invented, a seat for a square or baguette-cut stone has to be cut by hand. This procedure is a slow, step-by-step process and a true test of any jeweller's patience. The time and care devoted to this process has a direct effect on the look and feel of the finished piece. Some jewellers take this seating process one step further by opening out the row of pilot holes on the reverse of the piece to create a series of decorative back holes. A row of beautifully executed back holes is visually pleasing, but more importantly it reveals the amount of time and care the jeweller has dedicated to perfecting the mount and is a clear indication of the quality of the piece.

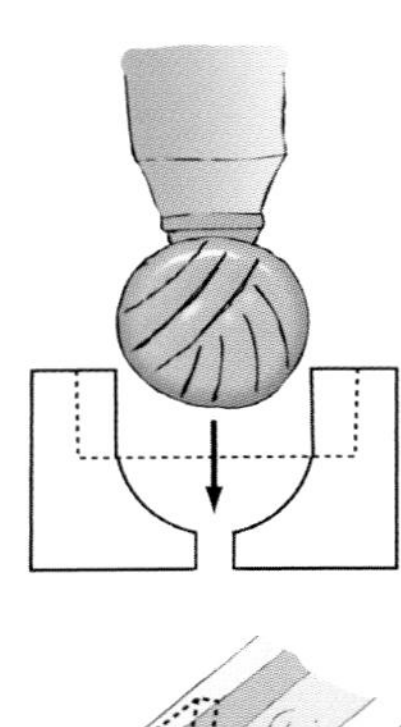

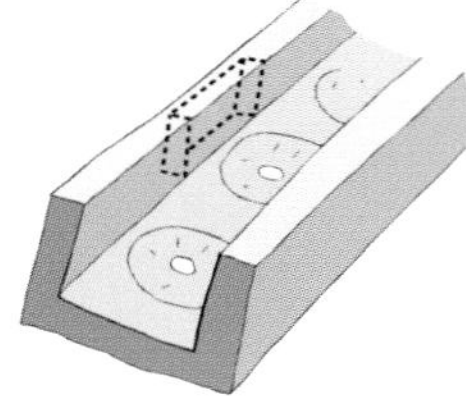

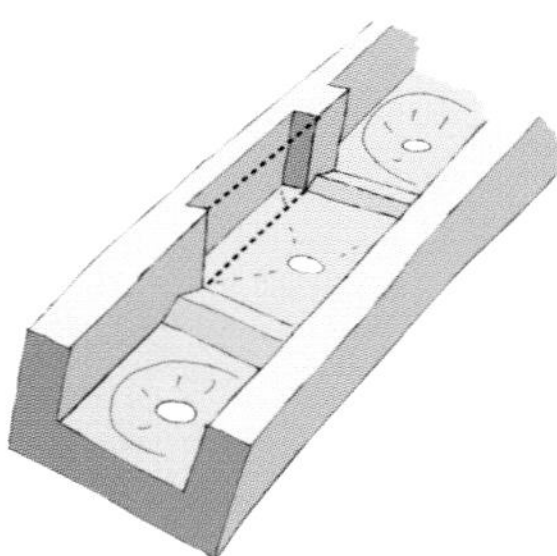

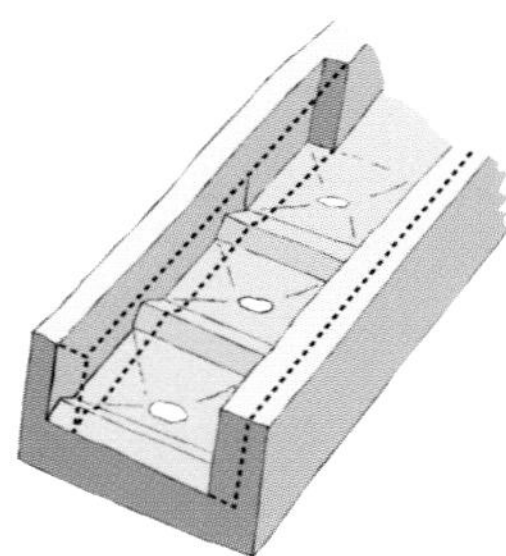

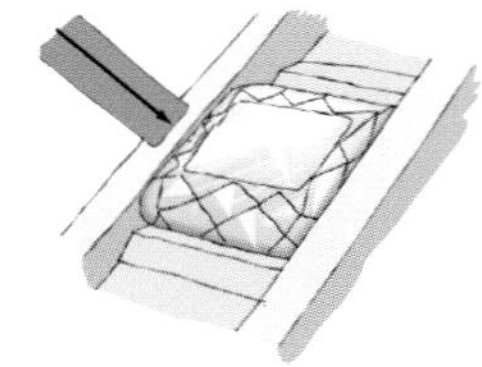

calibré

Calibré is the official term given to a group of straight-sided stones with the same uniform cut. A channel mount set with square, baguette or even emerald-cut stones is often referred to in the jewellery trade as a calibré setting. Calibré-cut stones are ideal for channel setting because their straight sides allow the required close contact of the girdles inside the mount. When executed professionally the stones in a calibré setting appear as a sea of uninterrupted sparkle, giving the illusion of one continuous stone, making it difficult to distinguish one stone from the next.

Let us take a look at the processes involved in seating and setting a calibré of 2mm square faceted stones. The measuring and layout techniques described on p.74–5 in relation to round stones apply when marking out a channel for square-cut stones. Once this has been done the next step is to cut the bearers into the individual seats, and it is here where we resume the instruction.

seating a channel of 2mm square calibré-cut stones

▶ First the bulk of metal inside all the pilot holes is removed using a ball burr, the diameter of which needs to be a fraction smaller than the stones being set (for this example 1.8mm should suffice).

▶ Next, the seat in the centre of the channel is opened up square using a sharp flat scorper and must be cut to the exact dimensions and shape of the allotted stone. To do this, first the walls of the channel are cut so as to 'let in' the stone. Then the interior of the hole is cut square to form the bearer for the stone's pavilion.

- It is essential at this stage that the girdle sits flat and level in its seat; if rocking occurs, metal directly under the pivoting area must be cut away with a knife-edge scorper.

- Excess metal is sliced away from the corners of the seat, again using a knife-edge scorper. This action helps prevent the stone 'snapping' during setting.

- It is important at this stage to cut through the dividing walls and into the neighbouring seats, the purpose of which is to locate the bearer of the adjacent seats on either side before the first stone is set. This is done using a knife-edge scorper.

- Once this is complete, setting the first stone can begin. Using a flat-ended pusher the wall of the channel is slowly brought down onto the girdle of the stone. Pushing starts by tacking the four corners of the stone, and as with a classic rub-over each push is executed from alternate sides. Once the corners are secure the wall in between is brought down to lock the stone in its seat.

- The process of cutting, seating and setting is repeated for all the stones in the calibré until the channel is complete.

- A safety back file is then used to remove any setting marks and a final emery will complete the setting process.

9. tension

Niessing Spannring 'Color'. 18ct alloyed gold and diamond. Photo courtesy of Niessing.

One of the more innovative forms of setting in recent years is tension setting. This beautiful, elegant and unique method relies on the tension within metal to secure a gemstone within an open ring. The nature of this setting means only gemstones high on the Mohs scale of hardness, – between 9 and 10 – are suitable, as the setting relies on the natural strength of the stone to withstand the tension created by the metal ring. A few such stones would be cubic zirconia, diamond, moissanite, ruby and sapphire. A stone that has a Mohs number of less than 9 may not be able to withstand the pressure from this type of setting, and may fracture or even shatter.

The pioneers behind this remarkable technique are Niessing, a European jewellery design and manufacturing company based in Vreden in Germany.

this is Niessing's story on how their tension ring was born:

'The games with light have begun. Only masters of their craft can carefully sever a gold or platinum ring and spread the breach so that a brilliant-cut diamond can be clasped inside the gap. The inherent tension of the metal band securely holds the stone.'

in *The Discovery of Light*, Walter Wittek recalls the genesis of the original tension ring

Ideas for my artistic work often arise through the formal results of related projects. In the summer of 1979 I was working on models for a sculpture. My plan was to take a steel ring with a round cross section and combine it with a rectangular pane of glass. I had severed the ring and was preparing to insert the glass pane. This turned out to be a very demanding task. The steel surfaces had to be absolutely flat and could only touch the pane at specific points. Otherwise the glass would shatter sooner or later, sometimes several days afterwards.

One morning when I entered my atelier, I found shards scattered across the floor and the steel ring in their midst. I lifted up the ring. A dazzling ray of light caught my eye: a fragment of glass was still wedged between the ends of the ring. I immediately felt that I was entering unexplored territory. The idea for a finger ring was born. I experimented with larger fragments of glass, polished glass gems, synthetic stones and natural topaz. I tried construction steel, copper, and sterling silver for the ring's band. My initial experiments were with these simpler materials.

It took a long time before the idea had matured enough so that the serial production could begin in the tension ring's final form of platinum with brilliant-cut diamond. I never completed the sculpture that I had originally planned. Instead, I had created a sculpture for the hand. The intention isn't to boastfully display a valuable gem inside an open ring. I was more interested in expressing the full potential and poetry of a cut and polished diamond by allowing it to play with light.

Creating the alloy. Photo courtesy of Niessing.

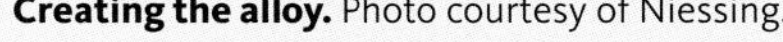

Forge strengthening. Photo courtesy of Niessing.

Niessing has produced Walter Wittek's Niessing Ring Round since 1981. In the ensuing years, the original form and principle has served as the basis for the development of an entire system of various Niessing rings.

'perfection through experience'

The statistics of each Niessing ring are impeccable. Each is crafted with cool perfection, a process beginning with fire and the glow of liquefied precious metal. For these rings Niessing developed special alloys that make it possible for the tension to be long-lasting and precisely targeted.

Lathe-opening the mount. Photo courtesy of Niessing.

Setting the diamond in place. Photo courtesy of Niessing.

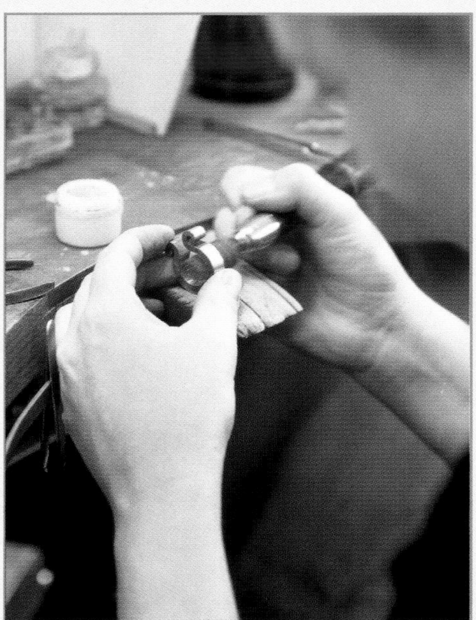
Cleaning at the bench. Photo courtesy of Niessing.

Experienced craftsmanship, manual dexterity and elaborate technologies are required to cut and widen the gap in the finished ring. Each of the various models poses its own unique challenges. The goldsmiths know each one like the back of their own hand. They measure the tension of each ring and then archive the empirically determined data so that the process used to manufacture each type can always be reviewed, even after many years have passed.

Each brilliant-cut diamond is individually tested to determine whether it can cope with the special demands of a Niessing ring. The stone must not have large inclusions in the wrong places; otherwise it could be damaged by the band's pressure, which can be as strong as 15 kg/sq. m. The gemstone setters shape the stone's 'bed' according to the peculiarities of the individual brilliant-cut diamond that will be inserted there. They ensure its ideal fit and consummate symmetry. The stone begins to float.

The techniques have continuously improved since the first Niessing ring. The manufacturing processes used in Niessing's workshops are subject to ongoing optimisation. More highly evolved techniques pave the way for designers to invent new shapes and new designs. Conversely, their novel ideas motivate the quest for new technical solutions. The various labours of the goldsmiths, diamond appraisers, stone setters, and designers all share one common goal: to create your personal Niessing ring.

Spannring **'HighEnd'.**
Photo courtesy of Niessing.

NIESSING RING 'HIGHEND'

The ring's opening continues outwards at almost a right angle. The flat planes guide the stone like twin protective tangents. They point towards the centre of the ring's circle, forming a gateway toward the interior. The balance between plane, angle, straight line and curve is perfect. The ring gradually grows thicker toward the bottom and retraces the line of tension. It's a bold construction for an opulent staging.

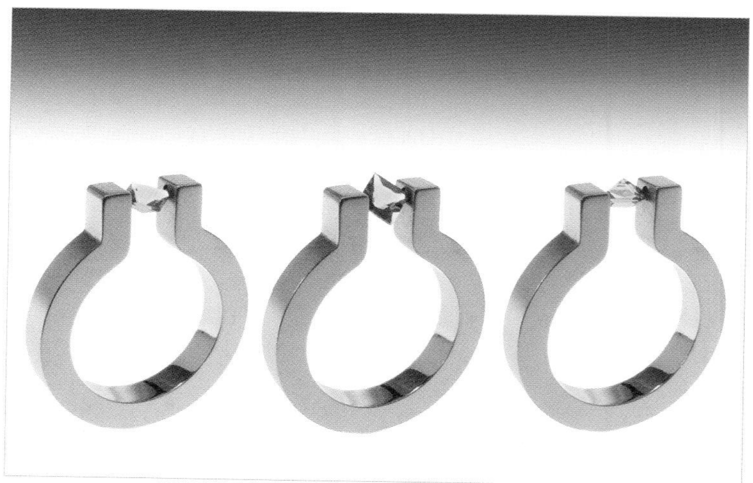

Angela Fung, Spin Ring Series. Titanium and citrine. Photo: Ashley Bedford.

The success behind the Niessing tension ring lies with the company's continual striving for perfection and design development, with a team of superior craftsmen repeatedly pushing the boundaries and constraints of the materials they use. This successful philosophy has paved the way for other jewellery designers to develop and investigate further the principles of the tension setting. One such designer is Angela Fung whose 'Spin Ring' series does just that.

the mount

The prepared shank.

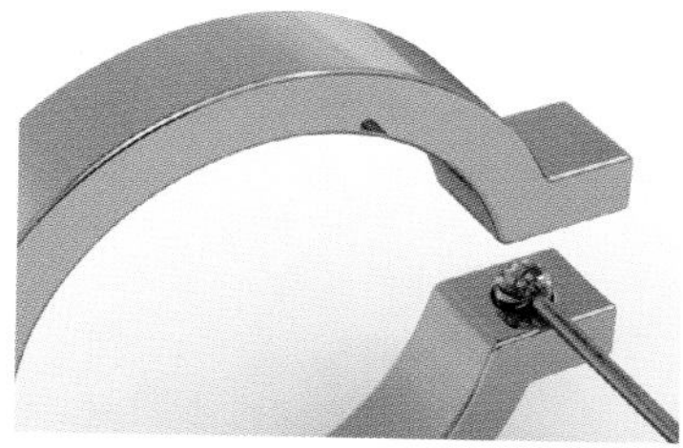

Creating the bearer using a ball burr.

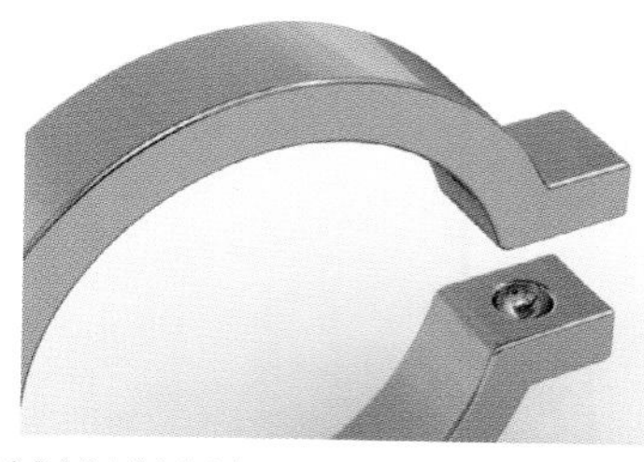

The mount ready to accept the stone.

Here Fung has swapped a precious metal shank for one of stainless steel. This shank is laser-cut from a solid block of stainless steel. This method of manipulation enables the shank to retain its natural tension, which is essential to the design. The shank is papered with fine emery and a high polish is applied.

The ring shank is now ready to be mounted.

Two holes are made on the inside of the ring's arms, using a ball burr and pendant motor. Accuracy in calculating the depth and positioning of these holes is crucial, allowing the stone to be positioned so as to be free to rotate with movement of the wearer's finger.

the setting

Once the burr holes are in place, the ring is ready to accept the stone.

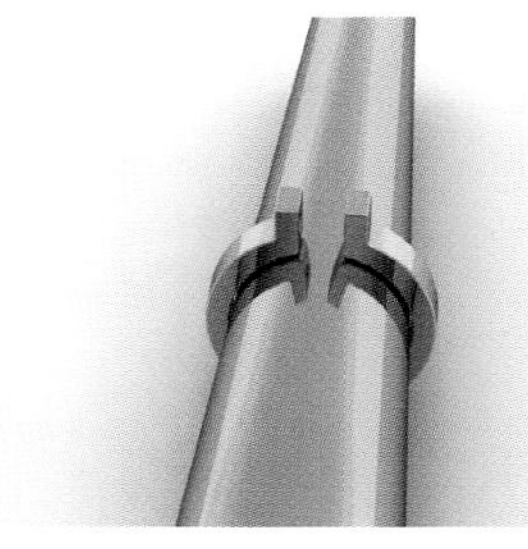

The arms of the shank are opened using a steel mandrel.

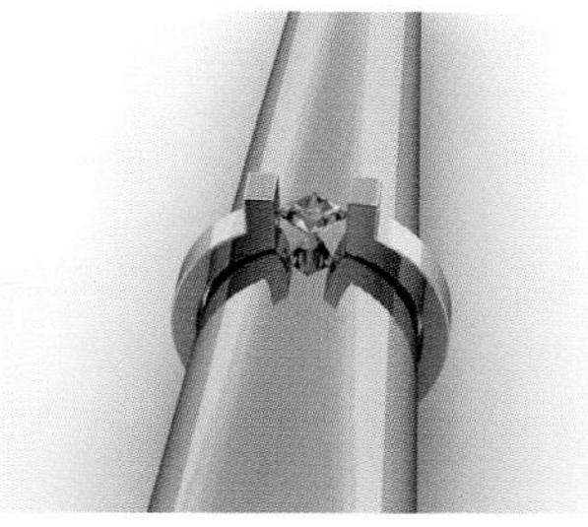

The stone is seated in position.

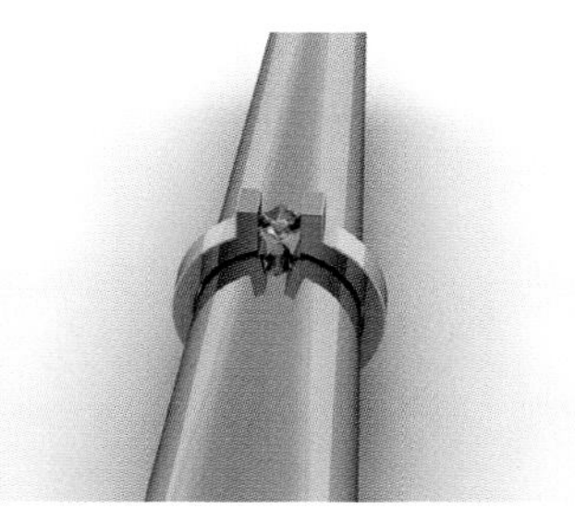

The stone is captured securely in the mount.

The ring is slid onto and encouraged down a steel ring mandrel. The arms of the shank open, allowing the stone to be dropped into position. The ring is then wriggled back up the steel ring mandrel. The arms then retract and trap the stone securely in place.

10. set from behind

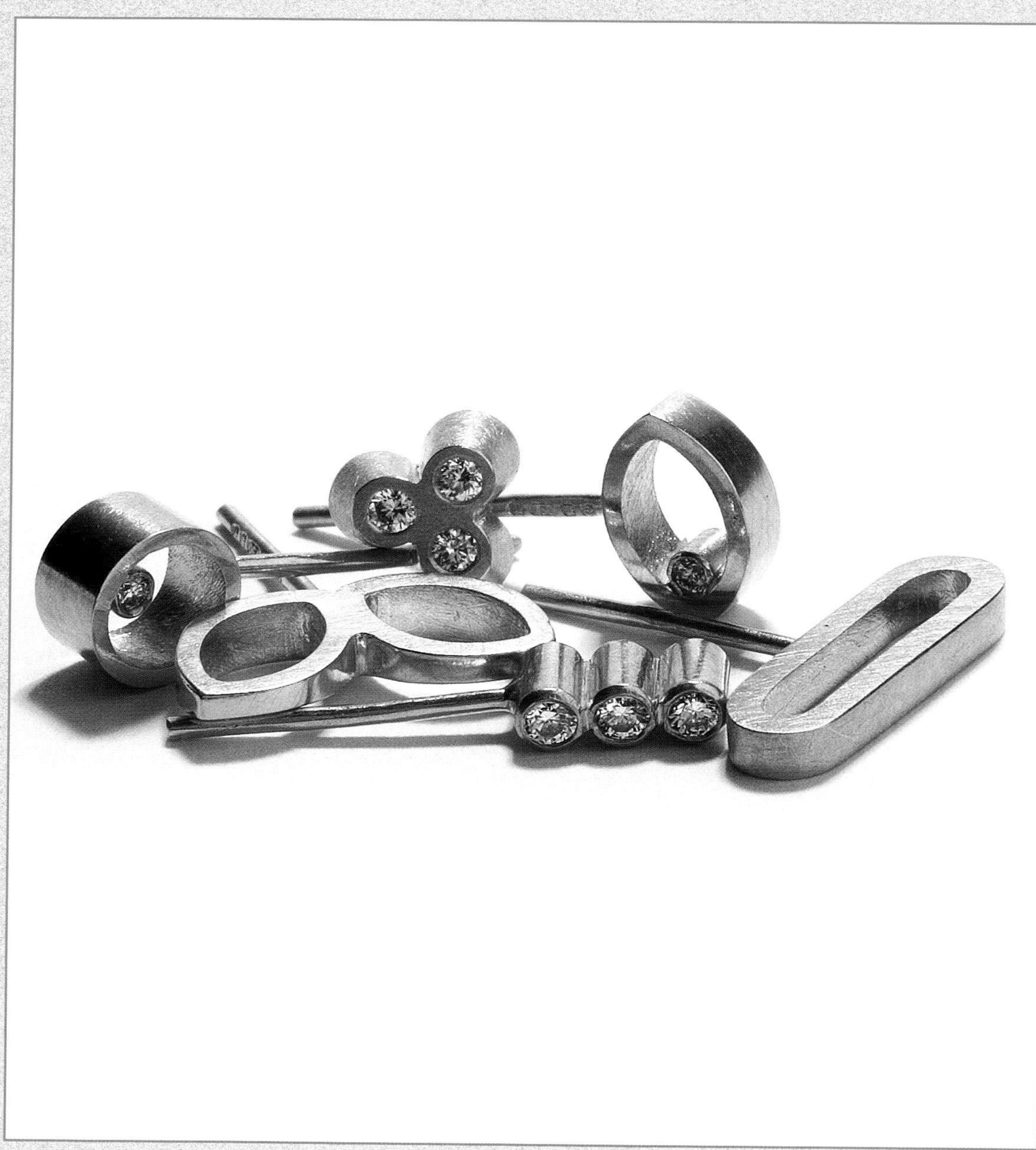

Amanda Doughty, diamond studs. 18ct yellow gold and diamond. Photo: Jeremy Johns.

This style of setting is perfectly suited to small round diamonds, given that a soldering procedure is required to secure the stone into its mount and diamond is the only stone that can withstand the high temperatures reached during the soldering process. However, diamonds are not indestructible, so the utmost care should be taken throughout the procedure. Always heat the piece slowly, evenly and with great care. Once soldered, leave the piece to cool down naturally, as quenching diamonds will almost always result in the internal crystalline structure being fractured, causing the diamond to appear cloudy.

If you are lucky enough to have access to a laser welder, then this form of setting is not limited to just diamonds – any type of stone can be used. This is because the laser emits an intense, direct heat that is hot enough to weld metal yet leave the stones themselves unharmed.

When executed with precision this style of setting leaves the front of the mount completely untouched, with a perfectly flat, crisp and clean finish, and the absence of any such marks can often confuse and intrigue the onlooker.

TIP

When preparing to solder, cover the diamond with watered ground borax. This will act like a thermal cocoon and help keep the diamond cool.

so how does it work?

The set stones are trapped in their mount from behind, leaving no visible evidence on the front of the mount that a setting procedure has taken place. As with the other setting styles we have looked at, the principles are the same, whereby the girdle of the stone is held in place. However, the significant difference here is that all the procedures are executed through the back of the mount and not the front.

the mount

The mount is constructed so that when the stone is placed on top, a thick wall of metal can be seen around the stone's circumference. The inside diameter, or bore, of the mount must be a fraction smaller than the diameter of the stone.

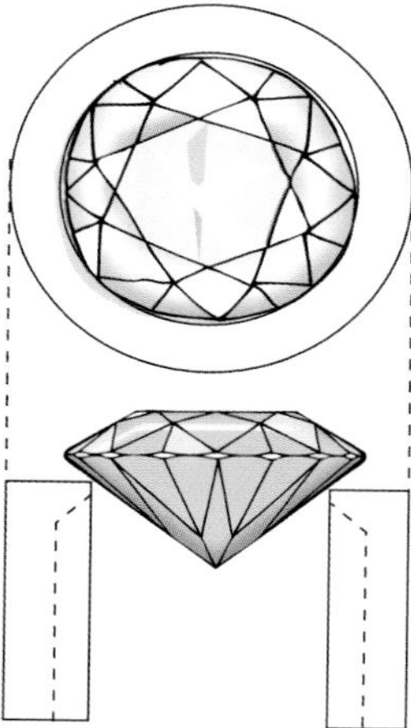

Thick-walled mount.

Next, a stone-setting burr, the same diameter as the stone, is used to create the bearer, though this time the burr is introduced through the back of the mount and not the front. Burring must stop just below the surface of the mount, which creates not only the bearer but also a bevelled rim that prevents the stone from falling out through the front.

The mount is now ready to accept the stone, which is dropped into position crown first – in this style of setting it is the crown side of the girdle that rests on the bearer, not the pavilion side. A gentle push from behind encourages a good position, and with the stone now seated the setting process can begin.

The burr mirrors the shape of the table of the stone.

TIP

To create the bearer and bevelled rim crucial to this style of setting the tip of the burr must mirror the angle of the stone's crown. The illustration opposite shows how a straight-sided stone-setting burr is ideal for this technique, though a ball burr or even a flame burr could also be used.

the setting

There are in fact several ways to secure the stone in its seat. One would be to raise tiny slivers of metal down the inside of the mount and curl them down onto the pavilion of the stone. Another is by inserting a wire bearer, with the exact internal dimensions of the mount, up behind the pavilion and soldering it in place.

A third method, as well as being the easiest to achieve, gives the most professional finish by far. A section of chenier, with an outside diameter (OD) to match the mount's newly burred inside diameter (ID), is inserted into the back of the mount and up behind the pavilion of the stone. Given the tight fit, the chenier and the mount are easily soldered together, trapping the stone in place.

This style of setting has to be one of the more rewarding, and with a little practice it can soon be perfected.

the example

The body of the pendant (below, left) is constructed from 14 equal sections of 18ct yellow-gold chenier with an internal diameter (ID) of 2.5mm and an outside diameter (OD) of 3mm. Each section is to be set with a single round brilliant diamond with a diameter of 2.6mm.

The step-by-step points opposite, together with the CAD illustrations below, are designed to help clarify the processes involved in achieving this style of setting.

18ct gold diamond cross pendant.

Burring the bearer from behind.

Inner tubes inserted to trap stones.

- The 14 sections of chenier are soldered in a cross formation using 18ct yellow-gold hard solder. The cross is then cooled and pickled.
- Then the pendant is placed face down and each section of chenier is burred from behind using a straight-sided stone-setting burr. The diameter of the burr must match that of the stone, so for this example the diameter will be 2.6mm.
- To create the bearer for the crown to rest on, burring must stop just below the surface of the mount, and the bevelled rim will prevent the stone from falling out through the front.
- When burring is complete the stones are dropped into position, crown first.
- Once all the stones are seated, the inner sections of chenier (OD 2.6mm) are inserted and pushed down onto the pavilion, trapping the stones inside the mount.
- To complete the setting process the second section of chenier is soldered in place.
- The back of the pendant can now be filed flush and the front may only require a light emerying.

11. a 'quick gypsy' solution

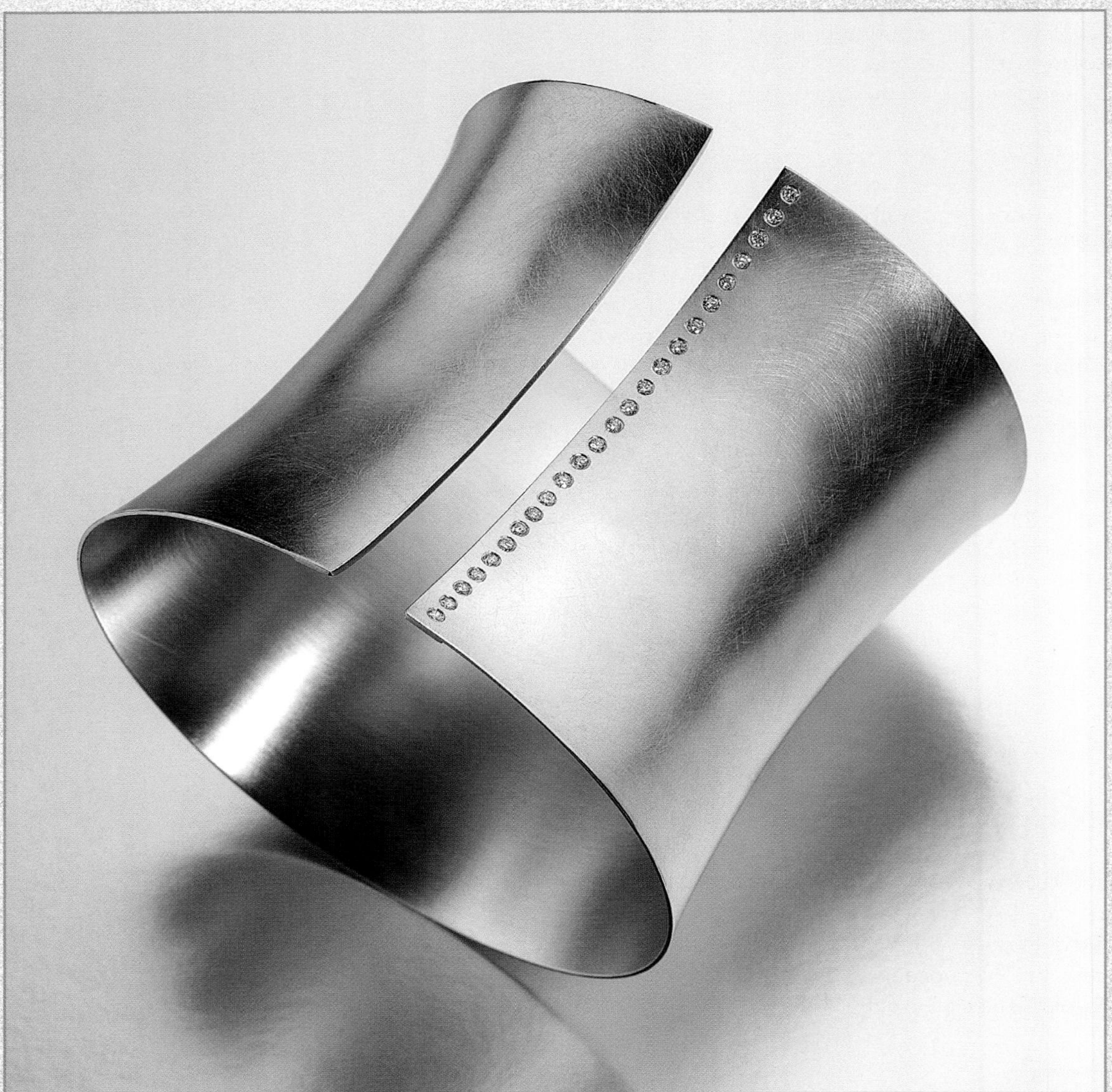

Sonia Cheadle, Platinum Cuff. Platinum and diamond.

Chapter 6, Gypsy, outlines the traditional method of this style of setting, and shows how the processes involved demand a high level of technical ability, concentration and tool control. The method explained below, however, is an adaptation of the traditional technique and can be easily achieved with a little practice. The processes involved in the 'quick gypsy' solution should boost skills and improve technical confidence, so that once you've mastered this technique you'll want to gypsy-set everything.

This method of gypsy setting can only be used to set small round faceted stones rated high on the Mohs scale of hardness, as during the setting process the table of the stone is used as a support for the steel setting burnisher. Diamond, ruby and sapphire are all suitable precious stones, while cubic zirconia makes an ideal alternative by adding a touch of sparkle without the great expense.

For this example a 1.75mm round cubic zirconia will be gypsy-set into a flat-section silver ring band. It is important to note here that for every different size of stone, a burr with the same diameter is needed. So for this example, our 1.75mm stone requires a 1.75mm stone-setting burr.

Ready-made ring bands and steel burrs can be bought from the larger bullion and tool suppliers, Cookson's in Birmingham probably stock the greater selection of both, while if you are looking to buy cubic zirconia, head to A.E. Ward in Clerkenwell in London. (See Useful Addresses at the back of this book.)

Before we get started, it is worth pointing out one small drawback to this method – a set of steel setting burnishers are required. Unfortunately, these cannot be bought and will have to be made.

However, do not let this put you off – a detailed description of how to do this can be found in the next chapter, Specialist Tools and Techniques. Besides, as we are looking at developing our personal skills set, why not add a session on tool making as well?

Let's take a look at how this quick gypsy solution works.

TOOLS AND MATERIALS USED

- ▶ Set of steel setting burnishers
- ▶ Sharp scriber
- ▶ Pair of dividers
- ▶ Small steel rule
- ▶ Selection of drill bits
- ▶ Hand drill
- ▶ Bench vice
- ▶ Stone-setting burr, with diameter to match the girdle of the stone
- ▶ Pin vice
- ▶ Stone tongs or steel tweezers
- ▶ A ready-made flat-section silver ring band
- ▶ Small round cubic zirconia with a diameter to match the stone-seating burr

a quick gypsy-setting solution

▶ As with the traditional style of gypsy setting the first task is to decide the position of the stone and drill a pilot hole. For this example a drill bit with a diameter of 1.5mm is used to create the pilot hole.

▶ Next, the bearer is cut to the optimum depth on the inside of the pilot hole using a 1.75mm stone-setting burr held in a pin vice. It is essential to this technique that the diameter of burr and stone are exactly the same.

The differential between the diameter of the pilot hole and that of the stone being set is very small. This is so because the burr need only remove a fraction of metal from the inside of the pilot hole to create a sharp tight seat. If this difference is too great then the burr would in fact be doing the job of a drill. Not only would this take an age, but the end result would be wobbly and uneven.

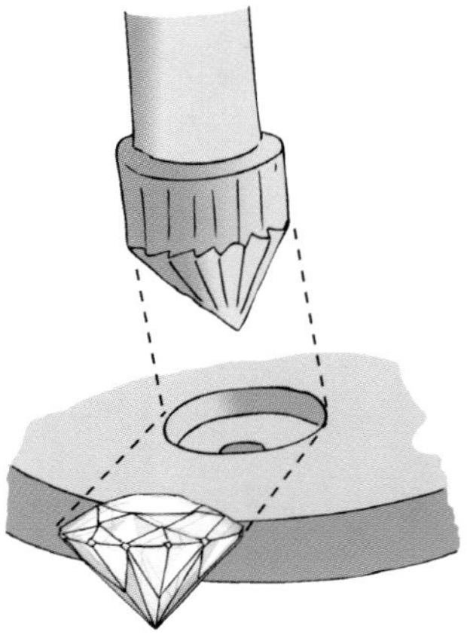

A pilot hole opened out with a stone-setting burr.

- For greater accuracy and precision when cutting the bearer, take the procedure slowly, remembering to gauge depth and position at regular intervals by testing the stone in the hole.

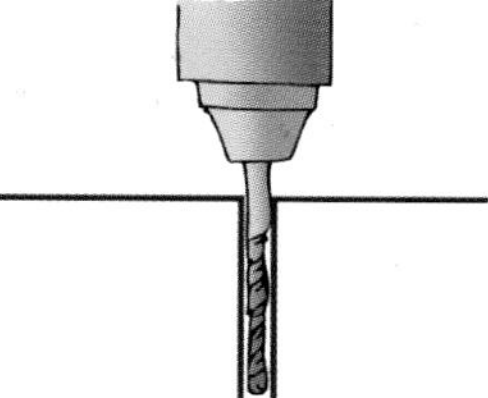

- Optimum depth has been reached when a sliver of the table can be seen when the ring is viewed across the horizon.
- The stone is now seated and ready to be set.
- Introduce the large round-headed setting burnisher into the channel, between the top of the table and the rim of the hole, at a 90° angle.

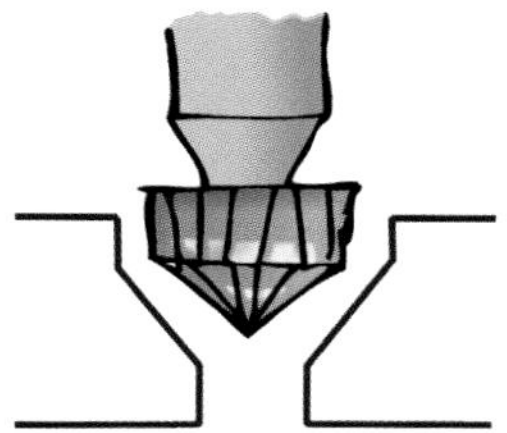

- A downward force is applied whilst the burnisher is slowly worked around the rim of the hole. Try to attain one complete revolution without removing the setting burnisher.
- Pressure from the burnisher flares the rim of hole, and after a few complete revolutions the rim will have collapsed onto the girdle and the stone should be locked in its seat.

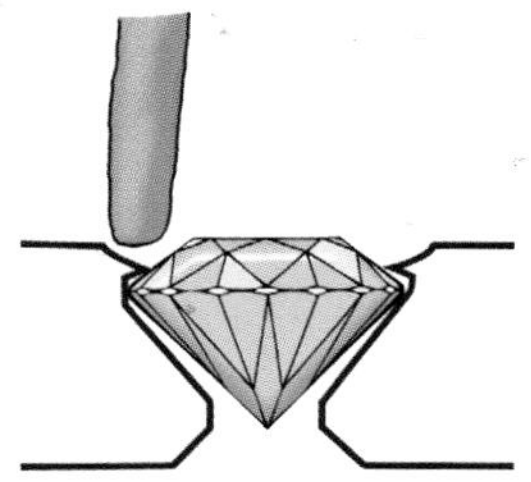

- When this has been accomplished take the pointed burnisher, again at 90°, and rub around the channel a couple more times to tighten the setting.
- The setting is now complete, though you would be strongly advised to check that the stone is secure with a firm push to the pavilion. If the stone breaks free, simply repeat the process starting with a gentle burr to remove the collapsed metal.

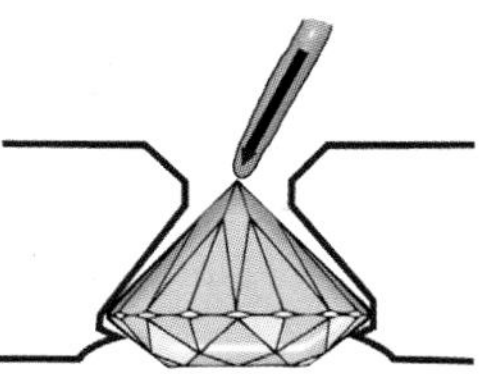

12. specialist tools and techniques

This chapter explores in depth some of the specialist areas mentioned in previous chapters. By using bullet-point guides and pictorial references the aim is to enable you to use and apply important tools and techniques with confidence in your own studios and workshops.

the mohs scale of hardness

1. Talc
2. Gypsum
3. Calcite
4. Fluorite
5. Apatite
6. Orthoclase
7. Quartz
8. Topaz
9. Corundum
10. Diamond

In 1812, the German mineralogist Friedrich Mohs devised the above scale as a guide to mineral strength and composition. Mohs based the scale on ten readily available minerals, with diamond, the hardest-known naturally occurring substance at the time, being placed at the top of the scale.

HOW THE MOHS SCALE WORKS

Each mineral listed in the Mohs scale will scratch all those with a lesser number and will be scratched by all those with a greater number. The scale is ordinal not linear, ranking the minerals from 1 to 10 but revealing nothing about the actual hardness of each individual mineral. For example, corundum (9) is twice as hard as topaz (8), but diamond (10) is almost four times as hard as corundum.

HOW IS IT USEFUL?

The scale plays an important role in the planning and construction of stone-set jewellery. Early identification of a stone's position on the scale will help inform the designer-maker which tools and procedures may cause damage. Procedures such as filing and emerying, setting and polishing should always be carried out with extreme care, as a tiny slip with a file or an overzealous polishing session could result in a damaged stone.

As a general rule of thumb, a stone with a hardness of less than 6 should never be touched with a file, buff stick or emery paper, because of the risk of scratching or even grinding the gem; and emery paper must be used with extreme caution around all gem stones, being predominantly composed of powdered corundum, which is rated 9 on the Mohs scale. This rule also applies to the polishing compound Tripoli, as Tripoli is an abrasive cutting compound made up of microscopic, microcrystalline quartz mined from beds of decomposed limestone, and is placed at 7 on the scale.

Diamond is the only exception to the above rule. As the hardest mineral currently known, diamond can only be damaged by another diamond. However, this does not mean that diamond is indestructible. Even though it cannot be scratched it may break or cleave if subjected to too great a pressure when being set.

It is therefore always advisable to exercise caution when working with any gemstone, whatever its hardness. A well-placed thumbnail can be used to cover and protect smaller stones during the delicate stages of construction. For larger stones, use masking tape to shield them against possible damage.

If ever the need arises to solder a piece of stone-set jewellery – say, as a repair or ring resize – the stones should ideally be removed before the process is carried out. Although a stone at the higher end of the Mohs scale (such as diamond, ruby or sapphire) should be able to withstand the heat required to carry out such a task, you should still take care. Moreover, make sure you always heat the jewellery piece slowly and allow it to cool naturally to avoid too sudden expansion and contraction. Never quench the item piece, as this will almost always result in damage to the stone's internal structure, causing a visual clouding of the stone.

As a useful guide, this list gives a few of the more commonly used gemstones, together with their Mohs scale ratings, available in today's jewellery market.

Agate	7
Alexandrite	8.5
Amber	2.5
Amethyst	7
Apatite	5
Aquamarine	7.5
Aventurine	7
Beryl	7.5
Chalcedony	7
Chrysoprase	7
Coral	4
Cornelian	7
Corundum	7.5
Diamond	10
Emerald	7.5
Feldspar	6
Fluorite	4
Glass	6
Haematite	6.5
Jasper	7
Kunzite	7
Lapis lazuli	5.5
Malachite	4
Moonstone	6
Morganite	7.5
Obsidian	5
Onyx	7
Opal	6
Pearl	3
Peridot	6.5
Quartz	7
Rhodochrosite	4
Rhononite	6
Ruby	9
Rutile	6
Sapphire	9
Spinel	8
Tanzanite	6.5
Topaz	8
Tourmaline	7.5
Turquoise	6
Zircon	7.5

And here are a few of life's everyday items placed on the same scale:

Fingernail	2.5
Gold, silver	2.5–3
Copper penny	3
Platinum	4–4.5
Iron	4–5
Knife blade	5.5
Iron pyrite	6.5
Hardened steel file	7+

bench-mounted grinder

A bench-mounted grinder is a good addition to any jewellery workshop, being the key piece of equipment when it comes to making tools. Check out your local DIY store to find the smaller, less expensive models. It's a great investment that need not cost the earth.

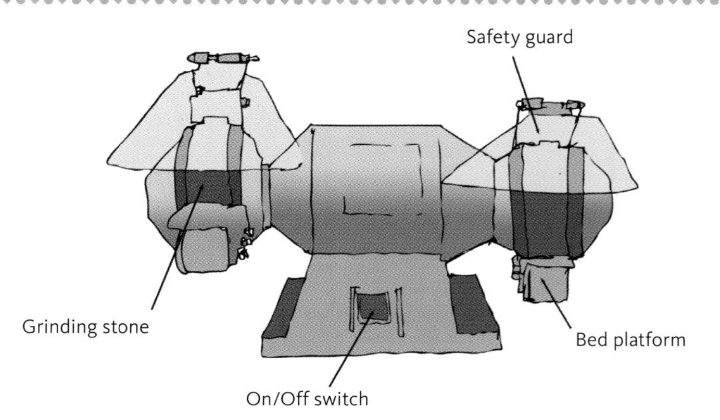

Bench grinder.

tools for a 'quick gypsy'

If the 'quick gypsy' solution is the answer to your setting needs then you will need to follow the steps outlined below to make a set of tools. Before we get started it is important to reiterate the simple but essential health and safety rules that must be adhered to when using any motorised machinery in a jewellery workshop or studio:

- Always protect your eyes with a pair of fully enclosed safety goggles or a pair of full-sided safety spectacles.
- Always protect your airways and lungs by wearing a face mask.
- Always tie back long hair and remove any loose items of clothing or jewellery that would be likely to get caught in rotating mechanisms.
- Always give a machine your full attention and operate with confidence as well as caution.
- Always adhere to the manufacturer's specified guidelines and always use any safety guards.

WHAT YOU WILL NEED

- Two lengths of tooling steel – for this example we will be using two discarded graining tools.
- Grinding machine – one from a local DIY store is quite adequate and won't break the bank.
- Coarse and fine emery sticks.
- Polishing mops – a bristle and a calico for the Tripoli and a swansdown for the Dialux polish.
- Polishing motor – preferably bench-mounted.

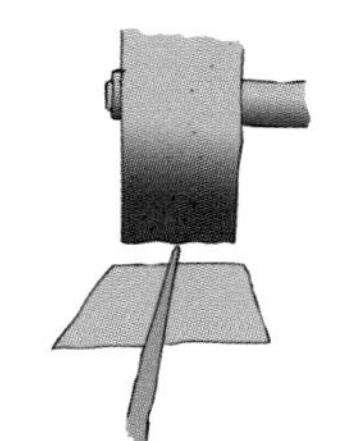

The tool on the bed at 90°.

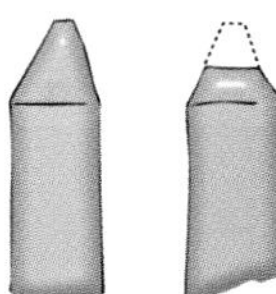

The tool before grinding (left) and after grinding, with a flat profile (right).

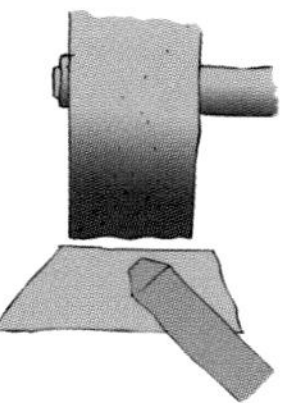

The tool on the bed at 45°.

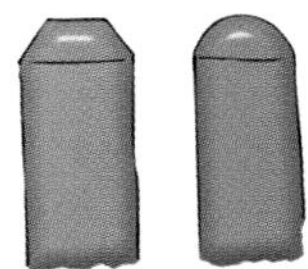

The tool before rounding the flat top (left) and with a new rounded profile after further grinding (right).

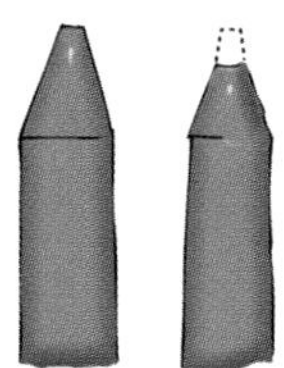

The tool before grinding (left), and after grinding with a blunt tip (right).

The two setting tools used to perform the 'quick gypsy' must have a specific profile for the technique to be a success. The first needs a large rounded profile while the second requires a pointed smooth tip. To help visualise the first when grinding, think of the rounded head of a doming punch; and when grinding the second, think of the writing tip of a ballpoint pen.

GRINDING THE FIRST PROFILE

▶ With the first old graining tool held flat on the bed of the grinding machine, introduce the end of the tool to the revolving wheel at an angle of 90°. Work the steel to reduce its tip by about half – this will create a flat-topped profile. To keep the tip cool whilst grinding, quench regularly in cold water.

▶ Next, the harsh edge of the flat top needs to be softened. To do this, holding the tool with one hand, introduce the harsh edge to the grinding wheel at an angle of 45°. When contact is made hold the position steady, and with the other hand carefully roll the tool on the spot one complete revolution of 360°.

▶ With the bulk of the steel now removed, turn off the machine and head to the bench. Use a coarse emery stick to smooth out any lumps and bumps, then to refine the profile move to a fine emery paper. The tool is now ready for polishing.

GRINDING THE SECOND PROFILE

▶ With the second old graining tool held flat on the bed of the grinding machine, once again introduce its tip to the revolving wheel at an angle of 90° and reduce by about a third, this time to create a small blunt end.

▶ Next, to soften the angle of the blunt tip, introduce the tool to the wheel at an angle of approximately 30°, and as before rotate the shank of the tool a complete 360°. This step should take hardly any time at all. Once complete, work through the different grades of emery paper to finely tune the tool.

POLISHING BOTH TOOLS

- Attach a fine bristle mop to the polishing motor, give the bristles a good feed of Tripoli, then with a sweeping action run the tip of each tool through the bristles until a satin finish has been achieved.
- Swap the bristle mop to a hard calico and repeat the above previous action. The tip of each tool should now be shining!
- Clean both tools thoroughly with detergent and dry them. Change the mop to a softer swansdown, apply a good feed of Dialux polishing compound, and then sweep each tool through the mop until a mirror finish has been achieved.

The tools are now ready to use. They will need to be resurfaced from time to time, to help maintain them, but this is an easy process. Starting from the emery stage, simply repeat the steps outlined above.

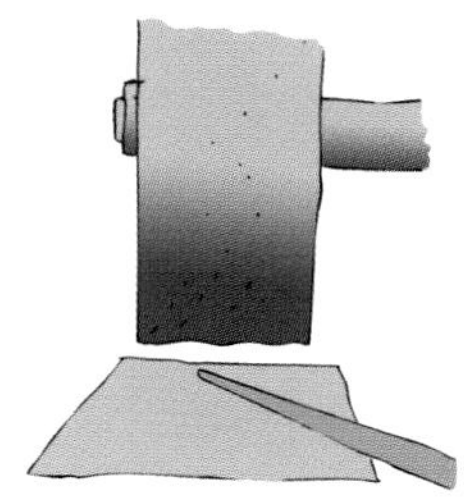

The tool on the bed at 30°.

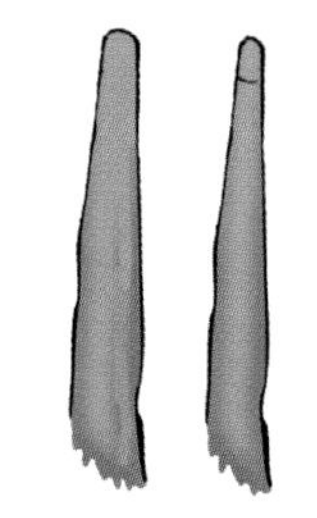

The new profile.

graving tools

A number of processes involved in mounting and setting require a range of cutting tools referred to in the trade as 'scorpers'. These tools feature quite heavily in the gypsy, pavé and channel styles of setting. The various scorpers mentioned throughout this book all have different uses, but the primary task they all share is to cut and slice metal.

To maintain accuracy and precision, the cutting face of each scorper has to be kept sharp. This is done by vigorously moving the cutting face back and forth across an oiled Arkansas stone at an angle of contact of between 30° and 50°.

The different types of scorper are illustrated overleaf alongside a brief explanation of their individual functions and a suggested method of sharpening.

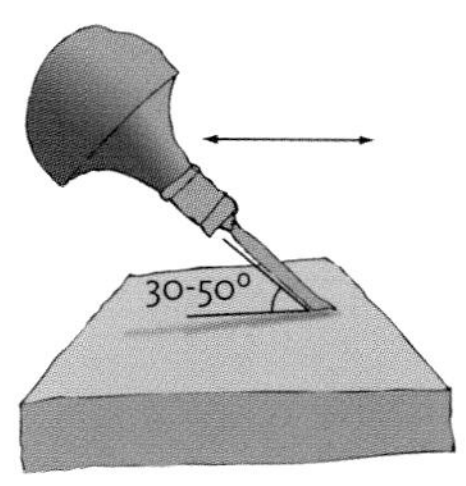

Arkansas stone and sharpening angle.

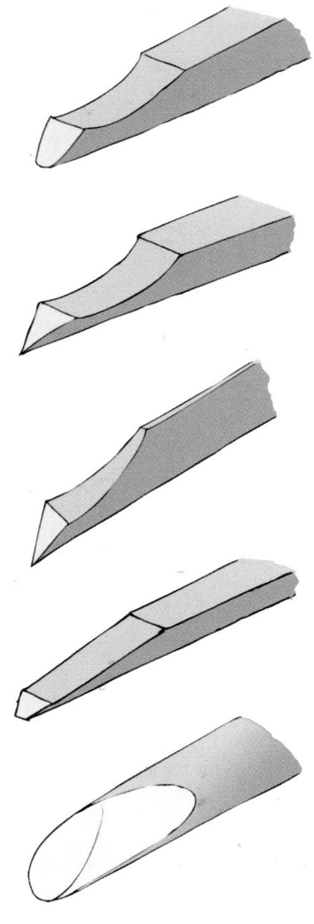

Half-round scorper

A half-round scorper is primarily used for raising grains in the pavé style of setting and is sharpened with the cutting edge facing away from you and perpendicular to the stone.

Knife-edge scorper

A knife-edge scorper is used for cleaning between grains in the pavé style of setting, and for cutting threads. It can also be referred to as a 'spitzstick', and like the half-round scorper it is sharpened with the cutting edge facing away from you and perpendicular to the stone.

Bright-cut scorper

A bright-cut scorper is used for cutting threads to brighten the metal surrounding an area that has been set. When sharpening, to achieve the correct angle, lean the body of the scorper toward you whilst moving it back and forth.

Flat scorper

A flat scorper is used to remove bulk metal when creating a channelled mount, and is also used for cutting bearers. It should be sharpened with the cutting edge facing towards you.

Bull stick

This is primarily used for cutting bearers and is sharpened leaning away from you, with its cutting edge facing towards you.

Burrs

A selection of steel burrs can usually be found scattered across jewellery benches around the globe. These tiny tools are instrumental to the processes of mounting and setting. A few of the more common ones are illustrated here.

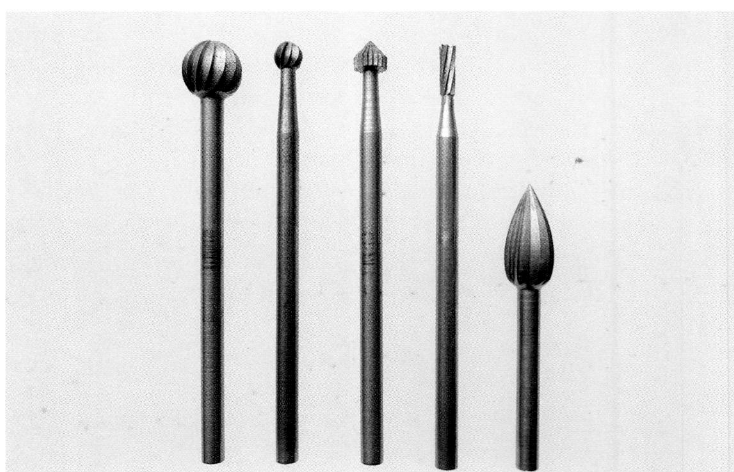

Burrs.
Photo: Sonia Cheadle.

A couple more tools that play an important role, but this time during setting procedure, are illustrated here:

Wax peg

A wax peg and a gemstone.
Photo: Sonia Cheadle.

Fashioned from beeswax and used for handling and manoeuvring gemstones.

Pusher

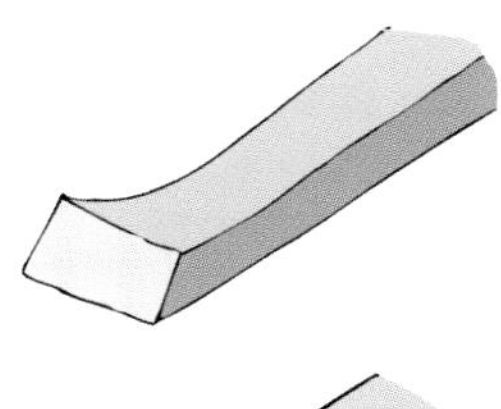

A flat-ended pusher is commonly used to push metal down onto the girdle of the stone during the setting process, to secure the stone in place.

Graining tool

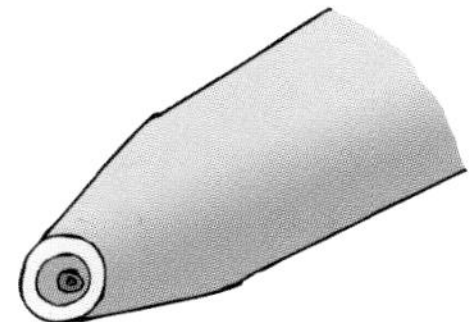

A graining tool is used to round off claws after setting or to burnish grains in between stones set in the pavé style of setting.

shellac

Shellac, more commonly referred to as setters' wax, is a hard, brittle wax with a distinctive burnt red colour. It is usually supplied as a small square brick set into an aluminium tray. The wax is removed from its tray, broken into smaller pieces, gently warmed, and fashioned onto the end of a wooden stick. The sticks are used by the setter to hold fast a mount during the setting process.
The following steps describe how a metal mount is set into a wax stick in preparation for setting:

TIP

An ultrasonic cleaning tank can also be used to help remove any excess wax. However, the crystalline structure of some gemstones cannot withstand ultrasonic waves that may damage or, worse, shatter the stone. Emerald, opal, pearl and turquoise, for example, should be kept out of the ultrasonic tank.

- Use the soft flame of a Bunsen burner to gently warm the surface of the wax to a consistency resembling putty.
- Take great care not to overheat the wax, as it will then become too runny to use.
- Gently heat the metal mount and sit it on the surface of the wax. The warmed mount should start to sink slightly.
- Using the sprung end of a pair of steel tweezers, tease the wax over the sides of the mount to embed and secure it.
- Quench the wax end of the stick in cold water and leave to cool.
- When the wax has hardened, the mount will be securely fixed and the stone can be set.
- After setting, gently reheat the wax to free the mount from the shellac.
- Soak the mount in methylated spirit to dissolve any excess wax.
- The setting is now complete and the finishing process can be carried out.

Setting sticks. Photo: Sonia Cheadle.

wrapping an emery stick

Emery sticks can be bought, ready-made, from the larger tool and bullion suppliers. This is, however, an expensive option; it is more economical to buy separate sheets of emery paper and wrap your own stick. When the working section becomes worn, just tear off a layer to reveal fresh emery underneath.

WHAT YOU WILL NEED

- ▶ 25cm length of rectangular-shaped dowel (approximately 16mm x 8mm cross section) from a local DIY store.
- ▶ Half an A4-size sheet emery paper
- ▶ Pointed scriber
- ▶ Elastic band

HOW TO WRAP AN EMERY STICK

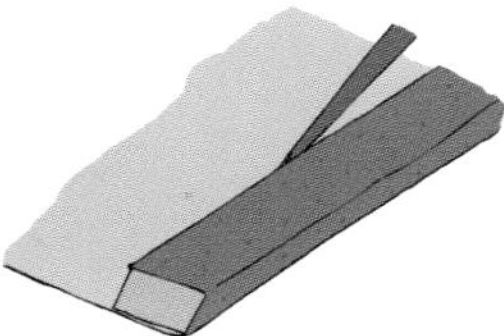

- ▶ Place the dowel across the emery paper, wide side down.
- ▶ Using a scriber, score a line on the emery paper the full length of one edge of the dowel.
- ▶ Fold the emery paper along the scored line.

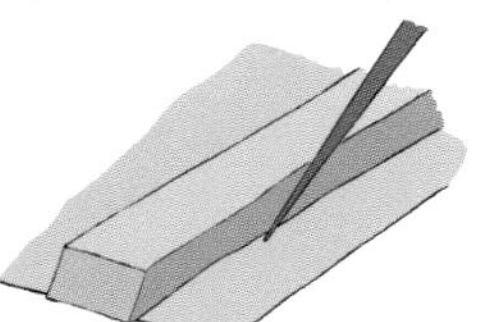

- ▶ With the stick held tight against the fold, score a second line down the opposite side of the dowel and fold the emery paper a second time.
- ▶ Turn the stick onto its narrow edge, scribe a third line and fold again.
- ▶ Repeat these steps until the whole sheet of emery is tightly wrapped around the stick.

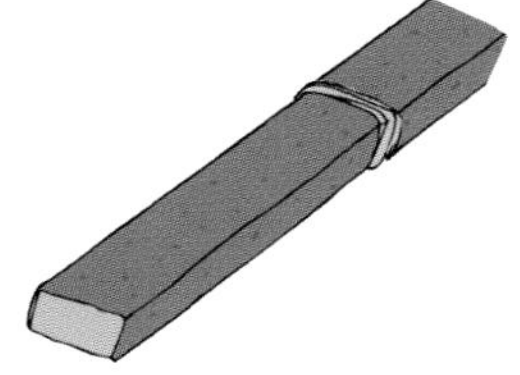

- ▶ Twist an elastic band around the middle of the stick to secure the emery paper in place.

binding wire

Binding wire is most commonly used to hold items together during soldering. Like all metals, binding wire also expands when heated as the tension within the metal is released when the heat source is applied. To counteract this expansion, relax the wire first by pulling it straight in between two sets of pliers, then use the relaxed wire to bind the items together.

Binding wire is also used to measure the circumference of a fancy-shaped stone, as it is easily fashioned around the girdle of the stone using a pair of snipe-nosed pliers. Once fashioned, the wire is then simply straightened out so the length can be recorded.

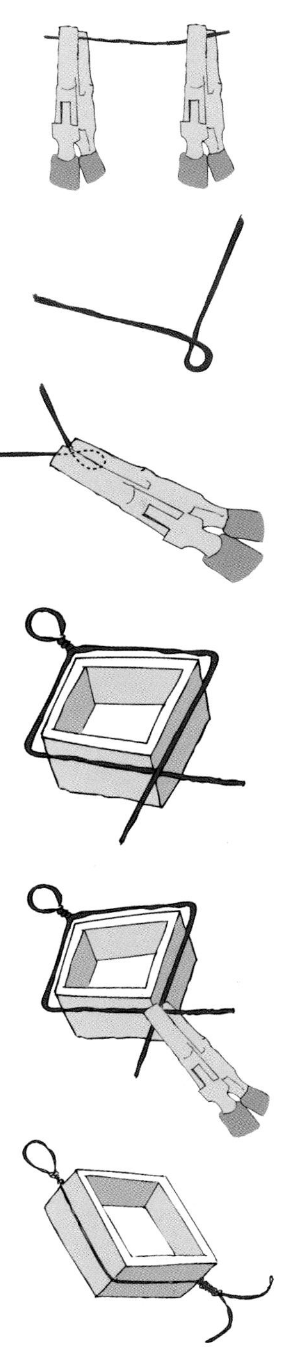

BINDING WIRE MEN

In Chapter 3, When Things Turn Fancy, binding wire is used to hold two halves of a mitred mount together during the soldering process. The technique used to create a binding wire shape, fondly referred to as a 'binding wire man', is outlined below:

- First pull a length of binding wire straight between two pairs of pliers.
- Then bend the wire in the middle and cross over the ends to form a small loop. Using a pair of flat-nosed pliers, grab the loop and twist a couple of times to form a 'head'.
- Next create the 'body' by fashioning the wire to echo the shape of the mount being held.
- Slip the body over the mount, then, to form the legs and to tighten the bind, use a pair of flat-nosed pliers and execute a couple more twists.
- The binding is now complete and the mount can be soldered.

gallery

This chapter is a celebration of work by some of the jewellery world's finest contemporary makers. They have all clearly mastered the art of mounting and setting, and some have dared to explore the conventional boundaries and challenge the normal constraints.

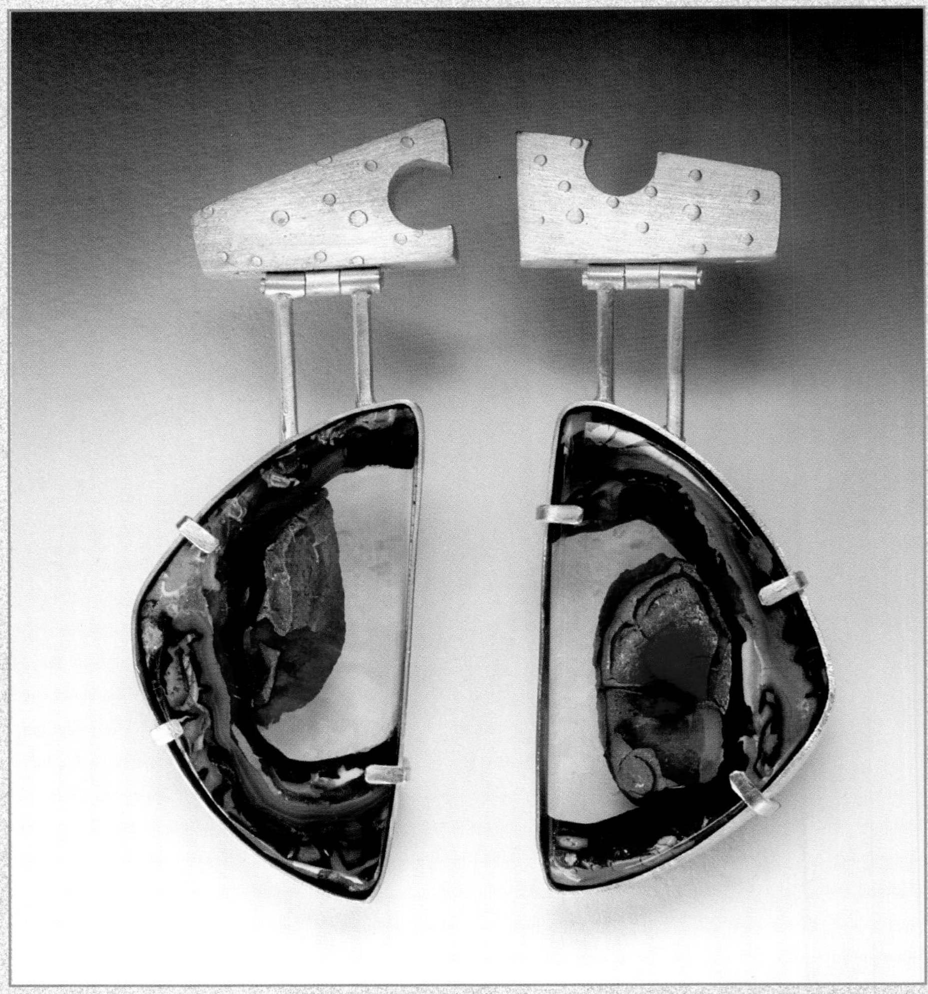

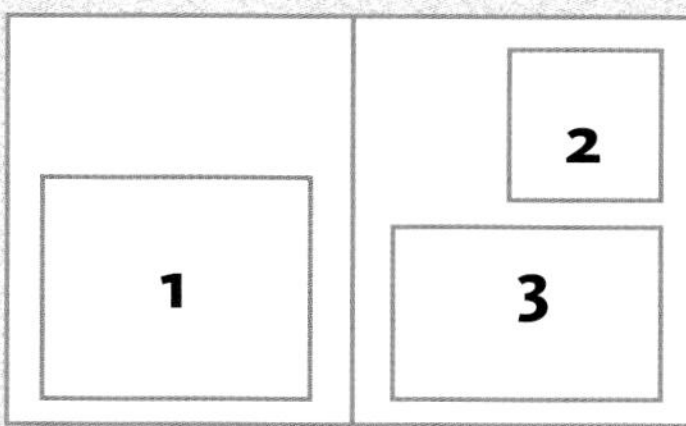

1 Barbara Christie, translucent opal drop earrings. Claw-set opals in 18ct yellow gold. Photo: Graeme Harris.

2 Barbara Christie, Cave Men Earrings. Green drusée with pink-brown crystals. Cast silver men claw-set in oxidized silver frames with crystal bead. Photo: Graeme Harris.

3 Barbara Christie, Oceans Necklace. Black drusée stone, set in 18ct yellow gold with cast 22ct gold penguins and ocean-blue tourmaline drop. Oxidised silver chain and hematite beads. Photo: Graeme Harris.

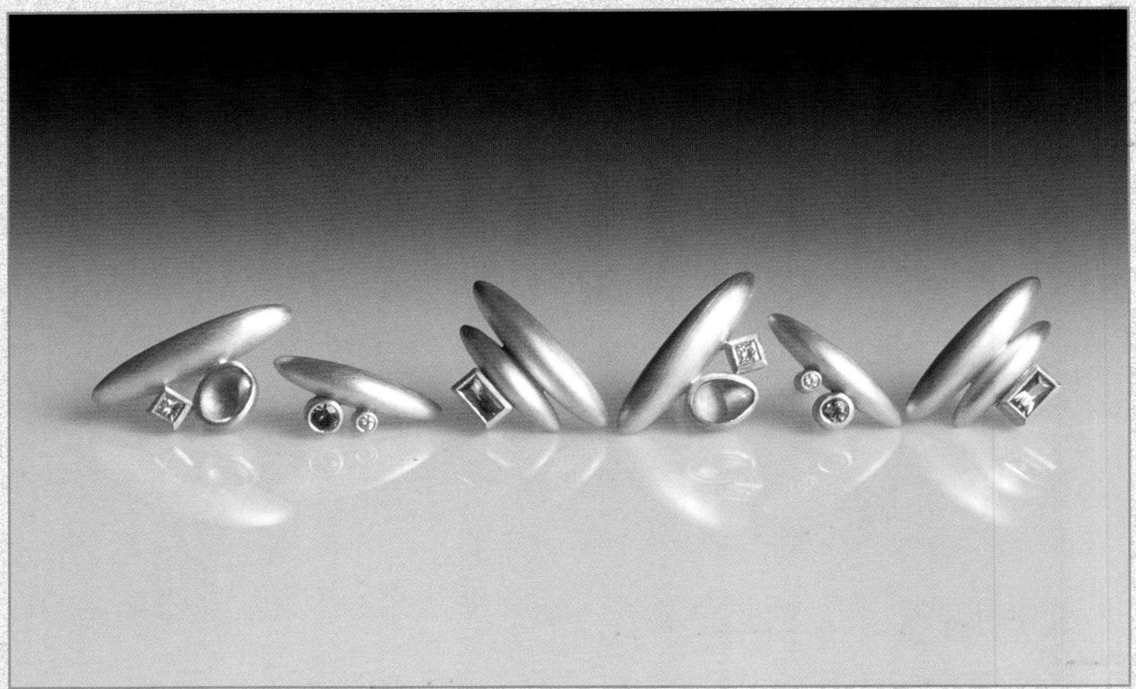

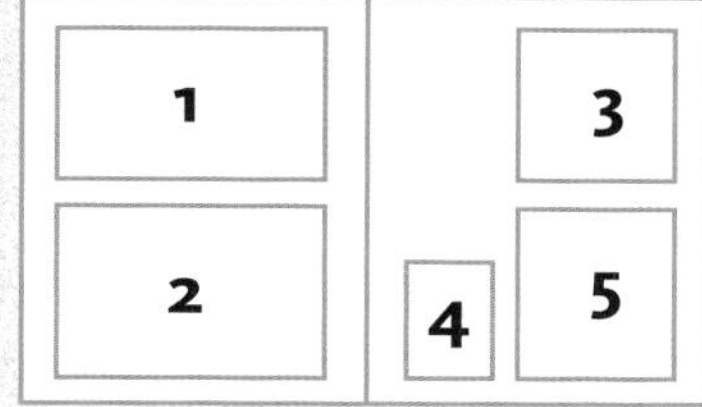

1 Mark Nuell, Silver Studs.
Pink tourmaline, diamond and sapphire.
Photo: FXP Photography.

2 Mark Nuell, Green Tourmaline Drop.
18ct yellow gold and diamond.
Photo: FXP Photography.

3 Cox & Power, Diamond Shards.
Platinum and diamond drop earrings.
Photo: Tim Kent.

4 Kelvin Birk, 2Claws Cluster.
18ct yellow gold. Photo: Joel Degen.

5 Kelvin Birk, Deluxe Ruby Ring.
18ct yellow gold and oval ruby.
Photo: Kelvin Birk.

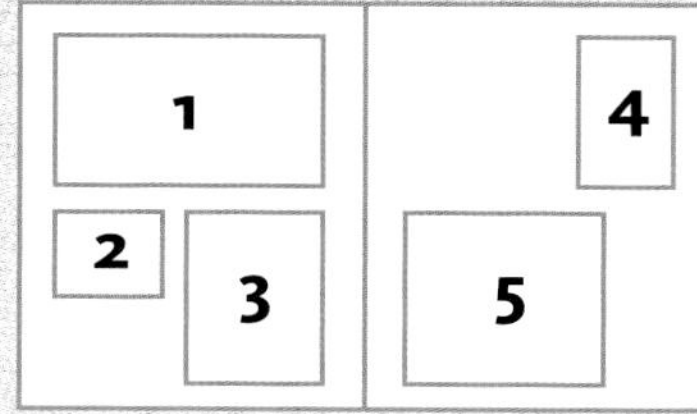

1 Herman Hermsen, Half-cube Rings. 18ct yellow gold and precious stone, silver and synthetic stones. Photo: Frank Kanters.

2 Herman Hermsen, Excentric Ring. Silver, tension-set synthetic stone, slot-carved on a lathe. Photo: Herman Hermsen.

3 Herman Hermsen, S-Ring Double. 18ct yellow gold and precious stones. Photo: Herman Hermsen.

4 Angela Fung, Globe Ring. Titanium, 18ct yellow gold, 12ct faceted amethyst. Photo: Ashley Bedford.

5 Angela Fung, Double Glide Bracelet. Titanium, 18ct yellow gold, blue topaz, peridot, citrine and amethyst. Photo: Ashley Bedford.

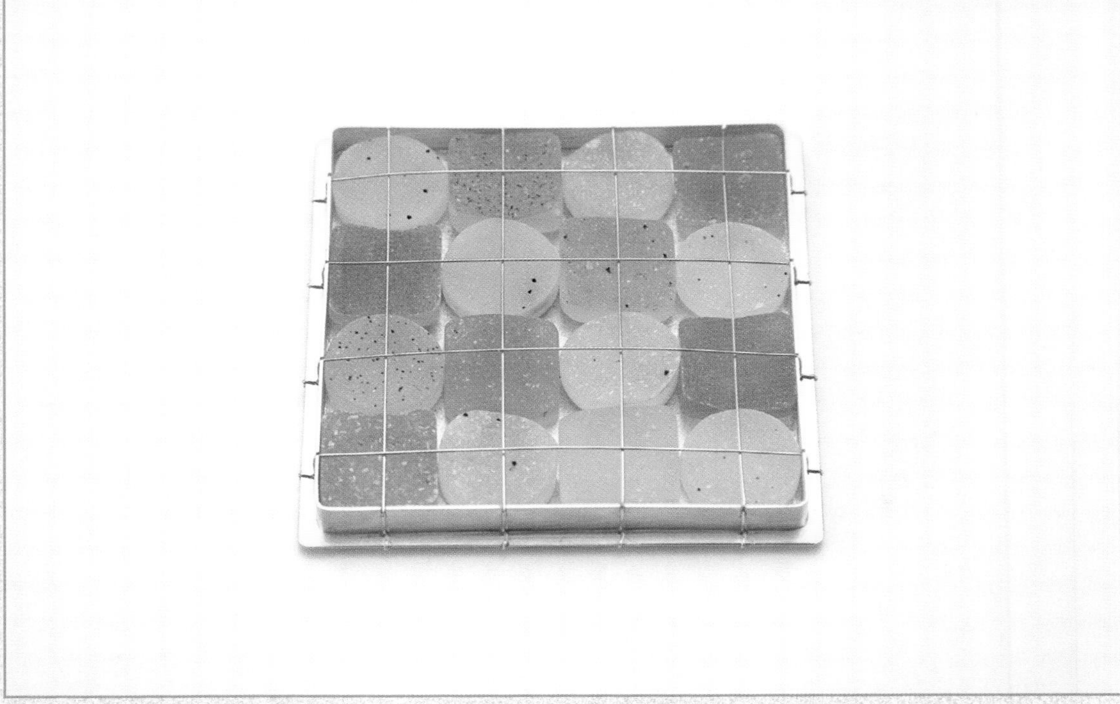

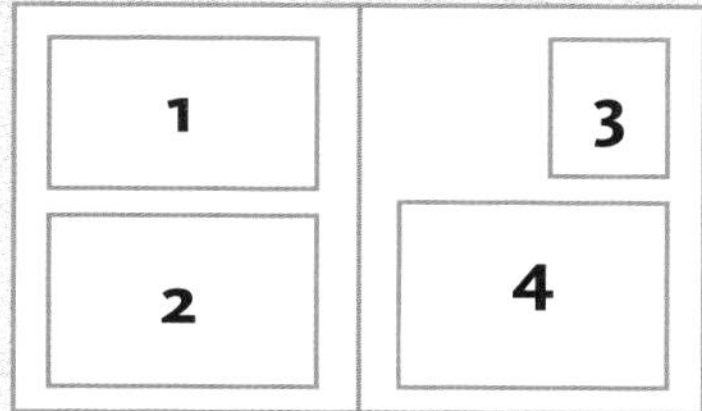

1 Etsuko Sonobe, Circle Brooch. 20ct yellow gold and claw-set agate stones. Photo: Shigeru Aoyagi.

2 Etsuko Sonobe, Square Grid Brooch. 20ct yellow gold and bound agate stones. Photo: Shigeru Aoyagi.

3 Etsuko Sonobe, Long Necklace. 18ct yellow gold and synthetic ruby. Photo: Shigeru Aoyagi.

4 Etsuko Sonobe, 18ct yellow-gold cage necklace. 18ct yellow gold and pink tourmaline. Photo: Shigeru Aoyagi.

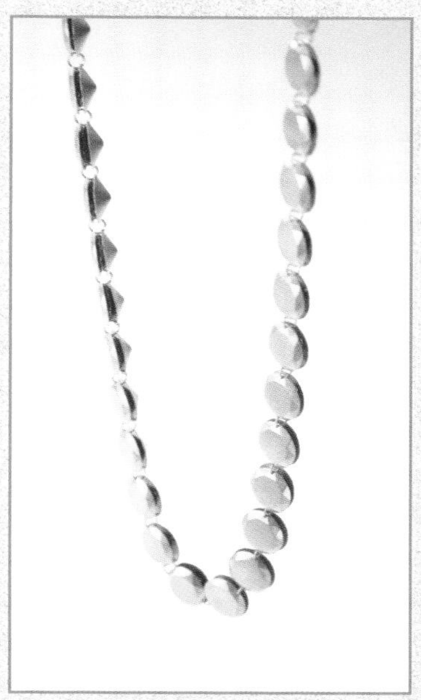

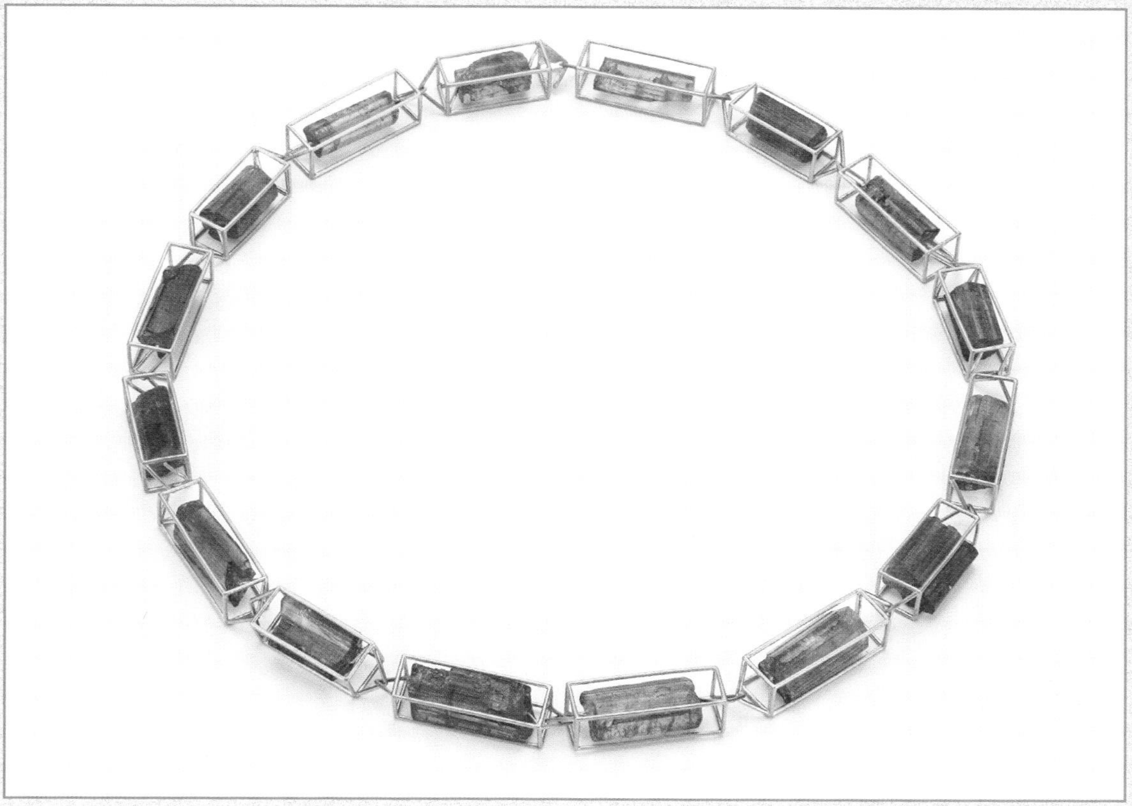

conclusion

Working with gemstones is a personal journey, one full of discovery and experimentation, successes and disasters, for which you will need resilience, an inquisitive mind and an endless supply of patience.

As each journey is unique, gather what you have learnt and then throw away the rule book: flip your stones, challenge the constraints of a mount, free your creativity and carve your own path. Be experimental, adventurous and explore; enjoy the journey and, very importantly, remember to record everything you find along the way.

This book is my journey. I hope it has inspired some but encouraged most.

useful addresses

Listed below is a selection of suppliers compiled from the recommendations of the jewellers included in this book. There are, of course, others. Several of the companies listed here sell their products online, and many operate a traditional mail-order service in addition to over-the-counter sales. Please note, however, that these are suppliers to the trade.

UK tool suppliers and bullion dealers

BELLORE
39 Greville Street
Hatton Garden
London EC1N 8PJ
Telephone: +44 (0)20 7404 3220
Fax: +44 (0)20 7404 3221
order@bellore.co.uk
www.bellore.co.uk

COOKSON PRECIOUS METALS/EXCHANGE FINDINGS
Birmingham branch (head office):
59–83 Vittoria Street
Birmingham B1 3NZ
Telephone: +44 (0)845 100 1122
or +44 (0)121 200 2120
Fax: +44 (0)121 212 6456
Birmingham.sales@cooksongold.com
www.cooksongold.com

London Branch:
49 Hatton Garden
London EC1N 5HY
Telephone: +44 (0)20 7400 6500

EURO MOUNTS & FINDINGS LLP
Birmingham Branch:
3 Hockley Street
Hockley
Birmingham B18 6BL
Telephone: +44 (0)121 554 0111
Fax: +44 (0)121 554 0777
info@eurofindings.com
www.eurofindings.com

London branch:
Antwerp House
26–27 Kirby Street
London EC1N 8JH
Telephone: +44 (0)20 7831 6701
info@eurofindings.com
www.eurofindings.com

RASHBEL UK
24–28 Hatton Wall
Hatton Garden
London EC1N 8JH
Telephone: +44 (0)20 7831 5646
Fax: +44 (0)20 7831 5647
www.rashbel.com

H.S. WALSH & SONS LTD

Beckenham branch:
243 Beckenham Road
Beckenham
Kent BR3 4TS
Telephone: +44 (0)20 8778 7061

London branch:
44 Hatton Garden
London EC1N 8ER
Telephone: +44 (0)20 7242 3711

Birmingham branch:
1–2 Warstone Mews
Warstone Lane
Hockley
Birmingham B18 6JB
Telephone: +44 (0)121 236 9346
www.hswalshes.com

UK stone dealers

MARCIA LANYON LTD

PO Box 370
London W6 7NJ
Telephone: +44 (0)20 7602 2446
sales@marcialanyon.com
www.marcialanyon.co.uk
A fabulous collection of gemstones, pearls and beads. Viewing by appointment only.

MARCUS McCALLUM

Telephone: +44 (0)20 7405 2169
Fax: +44 (0)20 7405 9385
Offers a fantastic selection of gemstones, pearls and beads in a bright and airy showroom. Call to make an appointment.

A.E. WARD & SON LTD

8 Albermarle Way
London EC1V 4JB
Telephone: +44 (0)20 7253 4036
gemstones@aewgems.co.uk
www.aewgems.co.uk

R.M. WEARES & CO. LTD

PO Box 9
York YO30 4QW
Telephone: +44 (0)1904 693 933
gemstones@rmweare.com
www.rmweare.com

Glossary of terms

Arkansas stone
Abrasive stone used to sharpen tools.

Annealing
The process used to soften metal through the application of heat with a jeweller's torch.

Back holes
A series of hand-cut holes that are visible on the inside of a ring or on the reverse of a stone-set piece of jewellery.

Bearer
A small cut ledge, or formed wire, on the inside of a mount to seat the girdle of a stone.

Binding wire
Soft thin wire used to hold work together whilst soldering. Usually made from mild steel but also available in stainless steel.

Buff stick
A small stick with leather at one end, used for polishing.

Buff top
A gemstone cut with a faceted pavilion and a smooth polished convex top or crown.

Bullion
Precious metal in large quantities, or as sold in the jewellery trade – sheet, wire, grain, etc.

Burr *see* **Metal burr** *or* **Steel burr**

Chasing tool
Steel tool used to chase metal

Chenier
Another term for metal tubing.

Chequerboard
A gemstone cut with a smooth polished pavilion and a faceted crown.

Collet
A collar or enclosing band that holds an individual stone.

Collet block and former
A steel tool engineered with two parts: the female block and the male former. Available in a variety of shapes and used to true metal mounts.

Culet
A small cut face forming the bottom or tip of a faceted gem's pavilion.

Dividers
A tool similar to a drawing compass, used to mark set distances or for scribing circles on the surface of metal.

Emery paper
Abrasive paper used to remove file marks from the surface of metal.

Former *see* **Collet block and former**

Gemstone rough
The 'host' rock for a gemstone crystal.

Graving tools
Tools used for cutting.

Grinder
A machine for grinding.

Half-round pliers
The jaws of these pliers have one flat and one half-round bed. They open with a pivoting action and are used to ease metal in a circular movement.

Hide mallet
Soft-leather hammer-like tool used to shape metal.

Laser cut
A process of cutting sheet material to a desired shape using laser technology.

Mandrel
A tapered steel former cast in a variety of shapes and sizes, used for truing larger jewellery items such as bangles. Wooden mandrels can also be bought, and these are less expensive than steel ones.

Metal burr
The small amount of irregular metal left behind as a by-product of burring and drilling.

Micrometer
An instrument used for accurate measuring.

Millennium cut
A cut gemstone cut with a total of 1000 facets. Created to mark the year 2000.

Mitre
To prepare two sections for a crisp join or seam by using a hand file to remove the inside edge of the metal.

Needle file
Narrow files available in different sizes.

Parallel pliers
A handheld device used for holding metal, the jaws of which open in a parallel action.

Pendant motor
A portable rotating motor that takes different jewellery tools for burring, cutting, polishing and so on.

Pickle
An acid solution used to clean metal after soldering.

Pierce
Action of cutting through metal using a piercing blade fixed in a jeweller's saw frame.

Pin vice
A tool used for holding wire, drill bits or burrs.

Safety back file
A needle file with teeth on only one surface.

Scorper
A handheld cutting tool (see p.104 for different types).

Scriber
A pointed steel tool used to score metals.

Snipe-nosed pliers
Pliers with a tapered nose and jaws that pivot open and closed.

Solder
A non-ferrous alloy used to join silver, gold and platinum.

Soldering
The term used for joining metal together using an alloyed solder.

Steel burr
Small steel tool in a variety of shapes used to remove metal, often fixed into a pendant motor.

Swage block
A steel tool engineered with a series of curved channels graduating in size.

Triblet
A tapered steel former cast in a variety of shapes and sizes, used for truing mounts and shaping rings.

True
To make exact or correct alignment.

Ultrasonic tank
Device that uses high-frequency vibrations in a liquid bath to remove dirt and grease from metal.

Vernier gauge
A calipered instrument used for accurate measuring.

Vice
A device for securely holding work, either held in the hand or mounted on a workbench.

Bibliography

Books

Grether, P.A., *The Technology of Setting*
(Lausanne: Editions Scriptar, 1984), ISBN: 2880120454.

McCreight, Tim, *The Complete Metalsmith: An Illustrated Handbook*
(Worcester, MA: Davis Publications, c.1982), ISBN: 0871921359.

Wooding, Robert R., *Diamond Setting*
(Erlanger, KY: Dry Ridge Company, 1984), ISBN: 0961354518.

Untracht, Oppi, *Jewelry Concepts and Technology*
(London: Robert Hale, 1982), ISBN: 0709196164.

Rühle-Diebener-Verlag GmbH + Co., *Practical Goldsmith Mounting – Setting* (2nd edn, 1995), PO Box 70 04 50, D-70574 Stuttgart.

DVD

The Goldsmiths' Company, An Introduction to Diamond Setting, with David Basford (2008), a Goldsmiths' Company Technology & Training Masterclass.

Websites

www.acj.org.uk
www.khulsey.com
www.ganoksin.com
www.professionaljeweler.com

Index